1st Workshop on Nordic-Baltic Responsible Evaluation and Alignment of Language Models (NBREAL 2025)

Tallinn, Estonia
2 March 2025

ISBN: 979-8-3313-1886-4

Printed from e-media with permission by:

Curran Associates, Inc.
57 Morehouse Lane
Red Hook, NY 12571

Some format issues inherent in the e-media version may also appear in this print version.

Printed with permission by Curran Associates, Inc. (2025)

For permission requests, please contact the Association for Computational Linguistics at the address below.

Association for Computational Linguistics
209 N. Eighth Street
Stroudsburg, Pennsylvania 18360

Phone: 1-570-476-8006
Fax: 1-570-476-0860

acl@aclweb.org

Additional copies of this publication are available from:

Curran Associates, Inc.
57 Morehouse Lane
Red Hook, NY 12571 USA
Phone: 845-758-0400
Fax: 845-758-2633
Email: curran@proceedings.com
Web: www.proceedings.com

NBREAL 2025

The 1st Workshop on Nordic-Baltic Responsible Evaluation and Alignment of Language Models

Proceedings of the Workshop

March 2, 2025

Introduction

We are excited to welcome you to NB-REAL 2025 (Nordic-Baltic Responsible Evaluation and Alignment of Language Models), a half-day workshop focusing on the responsible evaluation and alignment of Large Language Models (LLMs) for Nordic and Baltic languages. The workshop was held on March 2, 2025, bringing together researchers and practitioners working on ethical benchmarks, culturally sensitive alignment datasets, and responsible LLM evaluation techniques for Nordic and Baltic languages.

The NB-REAL workshop aimed to address critical challenges in the development and evaluation of language models for Nordic and Baltic languages, with a particular focus on ethical considerations and cultural sensitivity. The program included a keynote presentation, three oral presentations, and three poster presentations, covering a diverse range of topics from cultural awareness evaluation to multilingual tweet analysis.

We received 9 submissions this year. Each submission underwent a rigorous double-blind review process, with three reviewers assigned to each paper. Our program committee, consisting of 9 dedicated reviewers, provided thorough evaluations and constructive feedback. After careful consideration of the reviews and discussions, we accepted 7 papers, while 1 paper was rejected and 1 was withdrawn, resulting in an acceptance rate of 78%. The accepted papers were presented either as oral presentations or posters, based on their content and format.

The workshop program featured three oral presentations covering important topics such as cultural awareness evaluation of Danish language models, crowd evaluation of translations, and the development of Danish idiom datasets. The poster session showcased three additional papers focusing on multilingual LLM evaluation, particularly for Baltic languages, and image-text relation prediction.

A workshop of this scale requires the dedication and support of many individuals, and we have many people to thank. We extend our gratitude to our program committee members for their thorough reviews and valuable feedback: Barbara Scalvini, Garðar Ingvarsson, Iris Edda Nowenstein, Kenneth Enevoldsen, Lars Bungum, Mathias Stenlund, Peter Ebert Christensen, and Steinunn Rut Friðriksdóttir. Their expertise and commitment were essential in ensuring the high quality of the accepted papers.

This workshop was organized as part of the TrustLLM project (the European Commission, grant agreement no. 101135671), an EU-funded initiative aimed at developing trustworthy large language models. We gratefully acknowledge this support, which made the workshop possible.

Finally, we thank all the authors who submitted their work to the workshop and all participants who contributed to making NB-REAL 2025 a success. Through their contributions, we have taken important steps toward establishing more responsible and culturally aware approaches to LLM evaluation and alignment for Nordic and Baltic languages.

Hafsteinn Einarsson, Annika Simonsen and Dan Saattrup Nielsen, Program Chairs

Organizing Committee

Program Chairs

Hafsteinn Einarsson, University of Iceland, Iceland
Annika Simonsen, University of Iceland, Iceland
Dan Nielsen, Alexandra Institute, Denmark

Program Committee

Program Committee

Lars Bungum
Peter Ebert Christensen
Kenneth Enevoldsen
Steinunn Rut Friðriksdóttir, University of Iceland
Garðar Ingvarsson Juto, Miðeind ehf.
Iris Nowenstein, University of Iceland
Barbara Scalvini, University of the Faroe Islands
Mathias Stenlund, University of Iceland

Invited Speakers

Annika Simonsen, University of Iceland, Iceland
Dan Nielsen, Alexandra Institute, Denmark

Keynote Talk

Aligning and Evaluating Language Models: Challenges for Low-Resource Languages

Dan Saattrup Nielsen and Annika Simonsen
Alexandra Institute and University of Iceland
2025-03-02 09:15:00 – Room: **Venue at Hestia Hotel Europa**

Abstract: This keynote presentation examines two crucial aspects of developing reliable language models: alignment strategies and evaluation frameworks. The first part will focus on language model alignment, particularly for Germanic languages, presenting recent work from the TrustLLM project. We discuss key challenges in ensuring reliable and ethically sound language models, especially addressing the scarcity of alignment data for low-resource languages. The second part will provide a comprehensive overview of language model evaluation approaches, from traditional benchmarks to emerging methodologies like LLM-as-a-judge. We examine evaluation frameworks with special attention to low-resource languages, highlighting both available resources and critical gaps in evaluation datasets. The presentation emphasizes the interconnected nature of evaluation and alignment in developing trustworthy language models.

Bio: Annika is a Faroese computational linguist and PhD student at the Department of Computer Science, University of Iceland. As part of the TrustLLM project, her research focuses on Germanic language model alignment, building high-quality training and evaluation data, and aligning models.

Dan is a Senior AI Specialist from the Alexandra Institute in Denmark. He has a PhD in Mathematics and has worked with AI within both academia and industry, with 5+ years of experience in low-resource NLP. He is the creator and lead maintainer of the European LLM evaluation framework ScandEval.

You can find Dan on platforms such as GitHub, Hugging Face, LinkedIn, Bluesky, etc. with the username **saattrupdan**. His website is `saattrupdan.com`

Table of Contents

Towards Multilingual LLM Evaluation for Baltic and Nordic languages: A study on Lithuanian History
Yevhen Kostiuk, Oxana Vitman, Łukasz Gągała and Artur Kiulian 1

Evaluating LLM Judgment on Latvian and Lithuanian Short Answer Matching
Yevhen Kostiuk, Oxana Vitman, Łukasz Gągała and Artur Kiulian 12

What's Wrong With This Translation? Simplifying Error Annotation For Crowd Evaluation
Iben Nyholm Debess, Alina Karakanta and Barbara Scalvini 42

Image-Text Relation Prediction for Multilingual Tweets
Matīss Rikters and Edison Marrese-Taylor 48

The Danish Idiom Dataset: A collection of 1000 Danish idioms and fixed expressions
Nathalie Hau Sørensen and Sanni Nimb 55

Program

Sunday, March 2, 2025

09:00 - 09:15	*Opening Remarks*
09:15 - 10:00	*Keynote Speaker: Annika & Dan*
10:00 - 10:30	*Coffee Break*
10:30 - 10:50	*Paper Presentation 1*
	DaKultur: Evaluating the Cultural Awareness of Language Models for Danish with Native Speakers Max Müller-Eberstein, Mike Zhang, Elisa Bassignana, Peter Brunsgaard Trolle and Rob Van Der Goot
10:50 - 11:10	*Paper Presentation 2*
	What's Wrong With This Translation? Simplifying Error Annotation For Crowd Evaluation Iben Nyholm Debess, Alina Karakanta and Barbara Scalvini
11:10 - 11:30	*Paper Presentation 3*
	The Danish Idiom Dataset: A collection of 1000 Danish idioms and fixed expressions Nathalie Hau Sørensen and Sanni Nimb
11:30 - 11:40	*Closing Remarks and Future Directions*
11:40 - 13:00	*Poster Presentations*

Towards Multilingual LLM Evaluation for Baltic and Nordic languages: A study on Lithuanian History

Yevhen Kostiuk[1,2]
[1]ARG-tech,
University of Dundee
[2]OpenBabylon
ykostiuk001@dundee.ac.uk

Oxana Vitman
University of Bremen

Łukasz Gagała
Georg-August
Universität Göttingen

Artur Kiulian
OpenBabylon

Abstract

In this work, we evaluated Lithuanian and general history knowledge of multilingual Large Language Models (LLMs) on a multiple-choice question-answering task. The models were tested on a dataset of Lithuanian national and general history questions translated into Baltic, Nordic, and other languages (English, Ukrainian, Arabic) to assess the knowledge sharing from culturally and historically connected groups. We evaluated GPT-4o, LLaMa3.1 8b and 70b, QWEN2.5 7b and 72b, Mistral Nemo 12b, LLaMa3 8b, Mistral 7b, LLaMa3.2 3b, and Nordic fine-tuned models (GPT-SW3 and LLaMa3 8b).

Our results show that GPT-4o consistently outperformed all other models across language groups, with slightly better results for Baltic and Nordic languages. Larger open-source models like QWEN2.5 72b and LLaMa3.1 70b performed well but showed weaker alignment with Baltic languages. Smaller models (Mistral Nemo 12b, LLaMa3.2 3b, QWEN 7B, LLaMa3.1 8B, and LLaMa3 8b) demonstrated gaps with Lithuanian national history related questions (LT-related) alignment with Baltic languages while performing better on Nordic and other languages. The Nordic fine-tuned models did not surpass multilingual models, indicating that shared cultural or historical context alone does not guarantee better performance.

1 Introduction

Large Language Models provide a functional framework for tackling various natural language processing (NLP) tasks, such as question-answering (Izacard et al., 2022; Dong et al., 2024), machine translation (Zhu et al., 2023; Kocmi et al., 2024) and so on. However, LLMs have shown less reliable results for low-resource languages (Ranjan et al., 2024; Sakib and Das, 2024) due to the smaller fraction of available data in comparison to English and a few other widely spoken languages.

Benchmarking multilingual LLMs across languages is essential for evaluating their capabilities. However, the availability of high-quality, culturally aligned datasets remains a challenge. This need for culturally aligned high-quality datasets becomes even more critical when evaluating historical knowledge, where ensuring linguistic and cultural fairness adds a layer of complexity.

Verifying comparability of the results on historical knowledge QA datasets requires that a single set of historical events is queried in all languages. The choice of that set is likely to be biased to events more represented in widely spoken languages. Conversely, events that are more region- or cultural-specific are less likely to occur in the benchmarks. Finding and addressing these gaps is important to improve the fairness of LLMs and highlight historical and cultural biases.

In this work, we focus on evaluating multilingual LLMs on Lithuanian and general history. Our goal is to determine how LLMs perform on Lithuanian history exam questions when prompted in different languages and explore the alignment between languages and historical awareness, particularly within the Nordic and Baltic language groups.

Our contribution is the following:

- We automatically translated publicly available Lithuanian history exam question-answering dataset into Nordic (Danish, Finnish, and Swedish), Baltic (Estonian and Latvian), and other (Arabic, Ukrainian, and English) languages and partially manually

Proceedings of the 1st NB-REAL Workshop 2025 - Nordic-Baltic Responsible Evaluation and Alignment of Language models, pages 1–11
March 2, 2025

evaluated it.

- We tested GPT-4o (OpenAI et al., 2024), LLaMa3.2 3b, LLaMa3 8b, LLaMa3.1 8b and 70b (Dubey et al., 2024), Mistral Nemo 12b (Jiang et al., 2023), QWEN2.5 7b and 72b (Team, 2024; Yang et al., 2024), and GPT-SW3 and Nordic-trained LLaMa3 8b (Ekgren et al., 2023) models and compared their achieved accuracy scores per language and its average per language group.

Our findings revealed that GPT-4o consistently outperformed other models across all evaluated languages and language groups on a dataset of LT-related and general history questions. Larger open-source models, such as LLaMa3.1 70b and QWEN2.5 72b, also demonstrated strong and consistent performance in all languages. In contrast, smaller models like Mistral Nemo 12b, LLaMa3 8b, LLaMa3.2 3b, and LLaMa3.1 8b showed notable gaps in their historical knowledge from a Lithuanian perspective, particularly with Baltic languages, despite Lithuanian being part of this group. The best performance was observed in the Nordic language group, suggesting that cultural or historical alignment alone does not ensure higher accuracy. Interestingly, the Nordic pretrained models failed to surpass the multilingual model.

The code and data are available in our GitHub repository[1].

2 Related Work

Pre-trained LLMs have exhibited a remarkable ability to encode and retrieve factual and common knowledge across different languages (Wang et al., 2023; Zhao et al., 2024). However, there is a notable variation in model performance across languages, with a strong shift toward high-resource languages (Qi et al., 2023), particularly languages with Latin scripts (Ifergan et al., 2024).

The datasets used for benchmarking multilingual LLMs are created using either one of the two approaches: human annotation (Kocmi et al., 2023; Goyal et al., 2022) or translating existing annotated datasets using LLMs (Lai et al., 2023).

Although datasets created by human annotators provide accurate translations and task-specific precision, they require considerable investment of both time and finances (Yang et al., 2019).

On the other hand, with an advancement of LLMs, the translation performance of automatic tools has been significantly boosted lately. For example, ChatGPT demonstrates fewer errors with the launch of the GPT-4 engine, even for distant languages (Jiao et al., 2023). The quality control research on the DeepL translation tool found that DeepL[2] performed well in terms of translation accuracy, fluency, and naturalness, reaching an overall semantic similarity score 94.13 (Linlin, 2024).

This improvement elevated the creation of benchmark datasets on various tasks. DeepL was used for creating the X-FACT multilingual factual knowledge dataset translated in 25 languages (Gupta and Srikumar, 2021). In the research (Thellmann et al., 2024), five well-known datasets of various tasks were translated by DeepL into 21 European languages. LLMs with different numbers of parameters were evaluated on newly introduced datasets. The authors observed that models generally achieve higher performance on Romance and Germanic languages compared to Slavic languages.

ChatGPT was utilized to translate the 158K English instructions into 26 languages, including 7 low-resource languages (Lai et al., 2023). The data was used to instruction-tune LLM for multiple languages using reinforcement learning from human feedback. The resulting framework, Okapi, was also evaluated on datasets translated by ChatGPT from English into 26 selected languages.

3 Methodology

In this paper, we investigate performance consistency of LLMs within Nordic and Baltic language groups on the Lithuanian history exams questions. We hypothesized that the LLMs perform better in this domain, when presented with questions in languages from Nordic and Baltic groups than from other due to the cultural, linguistic and historical similarities.

The methodology consists of two steps: *data preparation* and *models' benchmarking*.

Data Preparation. To test the hypothesis, we chose EXAMS (Hardalov et al., 2020) dataset. Specifically, we used samples that correspond to Lithuanian history. Each sample contains a ques-

[1] https://github.com/OpenBabylon/NoDaLiDa2025-LT-History-Eval

[2] https://www.deepl.com/

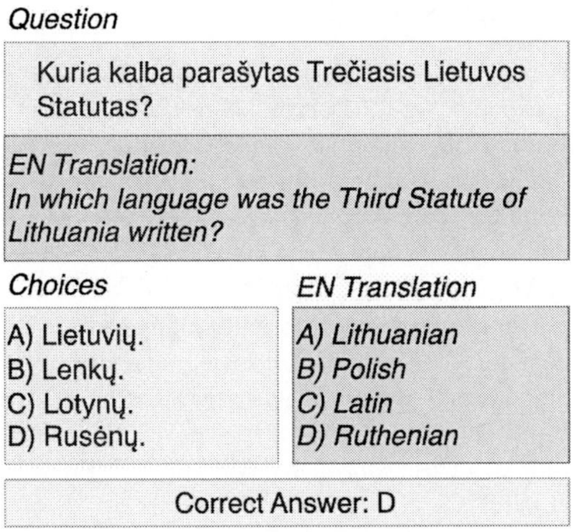

Figure 1: Example of the dataset sample in Lithuanian.

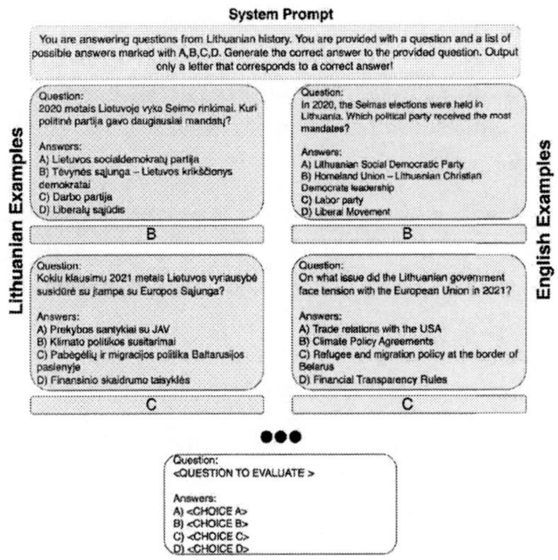

Figure 2: Example of the chat prompts that the model was presented to evaluate the dataset in Lithuanian and English languages.$< \ldots >$ is the actual question that the model is evaluated on.

tion, four different answer choices marked with the labels A,B,C and D with an indication of the correct one (see Figure 1). Questions and choices are in Lithuanian. We manually removed the questions that require an image to answer it, obtaining 550 samples.

The dataset was machine translated into Nordic (Danish, Finnish, and Swedish), Baltic (Estonian and Latvian), and outside of Nordic-Baltic, multilingual language group: Ukrainian, English, and Arabic. In more details, the dataset was translated from Lithuanian to English, and then the English translations were translated in other languages. We used GPT-4o (OpenAI et al., 2024) and DeepL as translation algorithms, as they are proven to have a good machine translation performance from- and to-English rather than between underrepresented languages (Wang, 2024; Hendy et al., 2023).

After that, we separated dataset into 2 parts: Lithuanian national history related questions (LT-related) and general history questions. We assigned a question to the LT-related group if it specifically mentions Lithuania, mentions Lithuanian historic figure or a question about the country that Lithuania was a part of or occupied by (e.g. Polish-Lithuanian Commonwealth, USSR after 1940 etc.). Other questions were assigned to a general history questions group.

To ensure quality, a subset of the dataset was evaluated manually by a group of native speakers. Annotators were presented with 100 English and translated language pairs (50 from LT-related and 50 from General history dataset) with 20 samples being the same for all the annotators to measure the annotators' agreement. For more details, see Appendix A.

Models' benchmarking. We experimented on the following models: LLaMa3 8b, LLaMa3.1 70b and 8b (Dubey et al., 2024), LLaMa3.2 3b (Dubey et al., 2024), Mistral Nemo 12b (Jiang et al., 2023), GPT-4o (OpenAI et al., 2024), QWEN2.5 7b and 72b (Team, 2024; Yang et al., 2024), and families of instruct pre-trained models developed by AI Sweden[3]: GPT-SW3 (Ekgren et al., 2023) (126m, 356m, 1.3b, 6.7b) pre-trained for and LLaMa3 8b fine-tuned for Swedish, Norwegian and Danish. GPT-SW3 models were pre-trained for Swedish, Norwegian, Danish, Icelandic, English, and programming code and LLaMa3 8b (we will refer to this model as NRD LLaMa3 from now on to avoid confusion) was fine-tuned for Swedish, Norwegian and Danish.

In our experiments, we used multilingual instruct LLMs. During generation, all the parameters were set to defaults, except for random seed, which we set to 2 with Ollama [4] framework for open source models. For Nordic models, we

[3]`https://huggingface.co/AI-Sweden-Models`

[4]`https://github.com/ollama/ollama`

used implementation from the *transformers* (Wolf et al., 2020). Specifically, we used GPT-SW3 and Swedish LLaMa3 8b[5]. The models were shown the same set of questions, translated to the corresponding language.

Another limitation of the approach is that we used GPT-4o for both translation and evaluation. To ensure that there is no data leakage, the model was shown only one sentence from the dataset at a time during translation and evaluation (along with manually crafted few-shot examples).

For each language in the translated dataset, the model was evaluated on the multiple choices question-answering task. The model was presented with a system message in English explaining the task, four question-answering examples in the corresponding language, and finally, a question with answer choices that the model has to answer. The examples were presented in the same format as the final question and consisted of question, four answer choices marked with A, B, C, D, and the correct letter for an answer as an expected output. Examples were taken from the modern (later than 2020) history of Lithuania, and do not intersect with questions in the dataset. Everything, except the system prompt, was presented to the model in the evaluated language (see Figure 2).

The results were parsed in the following way. If the model generated more than one letter, the generated text was separated into words. From these words, only capital letters were kept that corresponds to possible choice letters A,B,C, or D. If only one letter was present, it was considered as a final output. Otherwise, we assume that the model failed to produce a reasonable output and record it as if the model's answer was incorrect. As a result, we measured accuracy score for each model and each language.

During the evaluation, the translation quality can influence the final results. Since the original dataset was in Lithuanian, we would expect the models perform better on Lithuanian, as it did not go through translation steps. It is can be viewed as a possible advantage for Lithuanian over other languages, particularly for LT-related history questions.

[5] https://huggingface.co/collections/AI-Sweden-Models/

4 Results and Discussion

For each LLM, we grouped its results per language group into Nordic (Danish, Finnish, and Swedish), Baltic (Lithuanian, Latvian, Estonian), and multilingual (Ukrainian, English, and Arabic). The accuracy scores per language and averages scores per language group are presented in Tables 1 and 2 and on Figures 3, 4, and 5.

Our results demonstrated that all the models except for GPT-4o obtained better scores for general history questions rather than for LT-related ones. This observation is expected due to a biased training datasets for such models towards English-centric data.

The largest evaluated model, GPT-4o, performed consistently better than other models for LT-related and general history questions in all language groups. The model achieved a maximum average score of 0.88 for LT-related history questions for the Baltic group (BLT) and performed similarly for Nordic languages (NRD) with a score of 0.87, though it showed slightly weaker performance in the multilingual group (MLT), scoring 0.84. These results suggest better knowledge representation for Nordic and Baltic language groups in LT-related history exams. Among the individual languages, English and Lithuanian were the best-performing languages for both LT-related and general history questions.

The 70b group of models (QWEN2.5 72b and LLaMa3.1 70b) demonstrated second best performance across all the types of questions. QWEN2.5 showed lower accuracy for Baltic languages on average, obtaining similar scores for MLT and NRD groups. Also, in both types of questions, QWEN2.5 showed similar trends of receiving lower scores in Estonian and Latvian, but higher scores for Nordic languages. Additionally, its performance was better in general questions across all languages, but when it comes to the alignment with LT-related, model was able to output better results for English, Swedish, and Danish rather than for Lithuanian or Baltic languages. In contrast, LLaMa3.1 70b did not performed at par with diff language groups. The results are similar for all languages in all questions with Arabic being the weakest and Lithuanian with English slightly stronger than others.

In case of Mistral Nemo 12b, the model scored the smallest scores comparing to other, even smaller (7-8b, 3b) models. It showed similar re-

	NRD			BLT			MLT		
	LT	*G*	*LT+G*	*LT*	*G*	*LT+G*	*LT*	*G*	*LT+G*
GPT-4o	0.87	0.89	0.88	0.88	0.89	0.89	0.84	0.88	0.86
QWEN2.5 72b	0.74	0.87	0.81	0.71	0.83	0.77	0.76	0.87	0.82
LLaMa3.1 70b	0.72	0.82	0.77	0.72	0.81	0.76	0.72	0.81	0.77
M Nemo 12b	0.36	0.49	0.43	0.36	0.42	0.39	0.41	0.55	0.48
LLaMa3.1 8b	0.47	0.62	0.54	0.44	0.57	0.50	0.50	0.66	0.58
LLaMa3 8b	0.45	0.48	0.46	0.39	0.40	0.40	0.48	0.53	0.50
QWEN2.5 7b	0.49	0.62	0.56	0.46	0.48	0.47	0.58	0.73	0.65
LLaMa3.2 3b	0.40	0.50	0.45	0.34	0.33	0.34	0.42	0.47	0.45

Table 1: Average accuracy results per language group and model. **NRD** stands for Nordic, **BLT** stands for Baltic, and **MLT** stands for multilingual language groups. *LT-R*, *G*, and *LT+G* stand for Lithuania-related history questions, general history questions and merged history questions respectively. **M Nemo 12b** refers to Mistral Nemo 12b model.

	SW			DN			EN		
	LTR	*G*	*LTR+G*	*LTR*	*G*	*LTR+G*	*LTR*	*G*	*LTR+G*
NRD LLaMa3 8b	0.43	0.50	0.46	0.42	0.51	0.46	–	–	–
GPT-SW3 126m	0.27	0.22	0.24	0.27	0.21	0.24	0.27	0.20	0.24
GPT-SW3 356m	0.27	0.21	0.24	0.27	0.21	0.24	0.23	0.20	0.21
GPT-SW3 1.3b	0.23	0.24	0.23	0.23	0.23	0.23	0.23	0.24	0.24
GPT-SW3 6.7b	0.32	0.27	0.29	0.33	0.29	0.29	0.24	0.28	0.26

Table 2: Accuracy results for Nordic fine-tuned models. **NRD LLaMa3 8b** refers to pre-trained LLaMa3 8b by AI Sweden. *LTR*, *G*, and *LTR+G* stand for Lithuania-related history questions, general history questions and merged history questions respectively. **SW** (Swedish), **DN** (Danish), **EN** (English) indicate a language that was used for evaluating the model.

sults across all language groups, obtaining the same average accuracy scores (36%) on Baltic and Nordic group on LT-related questions and a better performance for Nordic group on general questions than for Baltic. The average of MLT group was better, even though neither score was higher than 64%.

LLaMa3 8b, QWEN2.5 7b, and LLaMa3.1 8b demonstrated a weaker performance when tested on BLT group across all questions. Using Lithuanian showed a better results. Similarly, Swedish and Danish helped QWEN2.5 7b obtain a better score. This results indicate that these models are better aligned with Lithuanian national history when asked in a language from Nordic group or in Lithuanian. LLaMa3.2 3b showed similar performance on NRD group to Mistral Nemo, but in MLT and BLT settings it received the lowest scores.

The Nordic-specific models performed similarly on all their supported languages. From the considered models, NRD LLaMa3 is a clear winner. It demonstrated a similar performance across its supported languages and is very close to LLaMa3.2 performance on Swedish and Danish, but still underperformed LLaMa3.1 8b and QWEN2.5 7b on the corresponding languages. When it comes to a family of GPT-SW3, the greater the amount of parameters - the better performance. GPT-SW3 6.7b outperformed other versions of the model across Swedish and Danish. However, on English, GPT-SW3 with 126m performed better on LT-related questions.

While our findings suggest that shared cultural or historical context does not guarantee better model performance, the other factors could potentially play a role. The evaluated multilingual models were trained on disproportionately larger datasets for Nordic languages due to its better availability (e.g. Wikipedia articles for Swedish and Danish etc.). This disproportion can explain the performance gaps, even for general

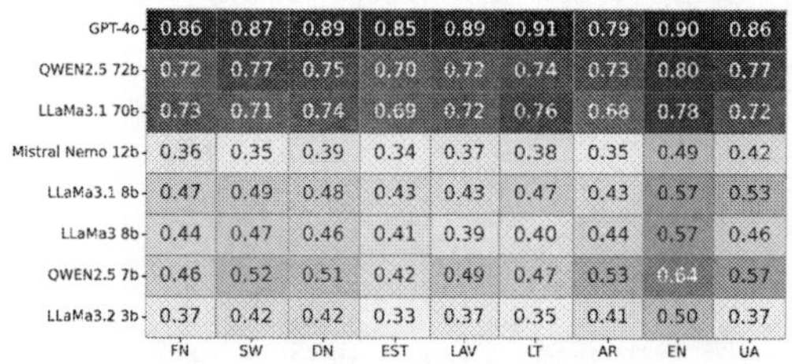

Figure 3: Accuracy results per language for LT-related history questions.

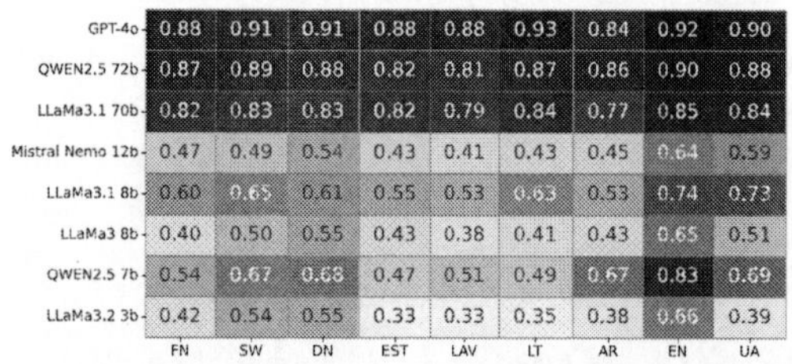

Figure 4: Accuracy results per language for general history questions.

knowledge questions. For instance, in our results, smaller models consistently achieved higher accuracy on Swedish and Danish compared to Lithuanian across both general and LT-related questions. These differences highlight the importance of training data availability and linguistic representation, in addition to cultural and historical alignment, in shaping LLM performance. Future work should further investigate the interaction between these factors to better address the challenges of underrepresented languages.

In conclusion, our experiments show that GPT-4o performs consistently better across all tested languages and language groups on LT-related and general history questions. Larger open source models, LLaMa3.1 70b and QWEN2.5 72b also performed consistently well in all languages. Mistral Nemo 12b, LLaMa3 8b, LLaMa3.2 3b, and

Figure 5: Accuracy results per language for merged LT-related and general history questions.

LLaMa3.1 8b demonstrated significant gaps in their historical knowledge for LT-related history questions within Baltic language group, even when Lithuanian is part of this group. The better performance was obtained in Nordic language group, indicating that cultural or historical alignment alone does not guarantee higher accuracy for these models. The Nordic pre-trained models were not able to outperform the multilingual model, rejecting our initial hypothesis.

5 Conclusion

This study evaluated the performance of Large Language Models (LLMs) on Lithuanian historical multiple-choice question-answering tasks, focusing on Baltic, Nordic, and other language groups. The models were evaluated on the Lithuanian national history related (LT-related) questions and a general history questions.

Our findings showed that GPT-4o consistently outperformed all other tested models across languages, achieving the highest scores for LT-related and general history questions, with slightly better results for Baltic and Nordic languages. Among open-source models, larger models QWEN2.5 72b and LLaMa3.1 70b performed well but did not match GPT-4o, especially in Baltic languages. Smaller models, including Mistral Nemo 12b, LLaMa3.2 3b, QWEN 7B, LLaMa3.1 8B, and LLaMa3 8b demonstrated weaker results with Baltic languages, including Lithuanian, while performing better in Nordic and multilingual groups.

Nordic fine-tuned models performed consistently across their supported languages but failed to surpass general multilingual models, even within their specialized domain. These findings highlight that shared cultural or historical context alone does not guarantee better model performance. To bridge these gaps, further efforts are needed to develop targeted datasets and fine-tuning strategies to improve LLM alignment with less-resourced languages like those in the Baltic language group.

Acknowledgments

This chapter is a product of the research conducted in the Collaborative Research Center 1342 "Global Dynamics of Social Policy". The center is funded by the Deutsche Forschungsgemeinschaft (DFG, German Research Foundation)—project number 374666841—SFB 1342. We would like to express our gratitude to the following organizations for their generous support, which made this work possible: GCP (Google Cloud) for providing credits used for model training and inference, and Tensorwave for providing AMD MI300X instance for inference and evaluations.

References

Mohamad Adam Bujang and Nurakmal Baharum. 2017. Guidelines of the minimum sample size requirements for cohen's kappa. *Epidemiology Biostatistics and Public Health*, 14:e12267–1.

Guanting Dong, Yutao Zhu, Chenghao Zhang, Zechen Wang, Zhicheng Dou, and Ji-Rong Wen. 2024. Understand what LLM needs: Dual preference alignment for retrieval-augmented generation. *CoRR*, abs/2406.18676.

Abhimanyu Dubey, Abhinav Jauhri, Abhinav Pandey, Abhishek Kadian, Ahmad Al-Dahle, Aiesha Letman, Akhil Mathur, Alan Schelten, Amy Yang, Angela Fan, Anirudh Goyal, Anthony Hartshorn, Aobo Yang, Archi Mitra, Archie Sravankumar, Artem Korenev, Arthur Hinsvark, Arun Rao, Aston Zhang, Aurelien Rodriguez, Austen Gregerson, Ava Spataru, Baptiste Roziere, Bethany Biron, Binh Tang, Bobbie Chern, Charlotte Caucheteux, Chaya Nayak, Chloe Bi, Chris Marra, Chris McConnell, Christian Keller, Christophe Touret, Chunyang Wu, Corinne Wong, Cristian Canton Ferrer, Cyrus Nikolaidis, Damien Allonsius, Daniel Song, Danielle Pintz, Danny Livshits, David Esiobu, Dhruv Choudhary, Dhruv Mahajan, Diego Garcia-Olano, Diego Perino, Dieuwke Hupkes, Egor Lakomkin, Ehab AlBadawy, Elina Lobanova, Emily Dinan, Eric Michael Smith, Filip Radenovic, Frank Zhang, Gabriel Synnaeve, Gabrielle Lee, Georgia Lewis Anderson, Graeme Nail, Gregoire Mialon, Guan Pang, Guillem Cucurell, Hailey Nguyen, Hannah Korevaar, Hu Xu, Hugo Touvron, Iliyan Zarov, Imanol Arrieta Ibarra, Isabel Kloumann, Ishan Misra, Ivan Evtimov, Jade Copet, Jaewon Lee, Jan Geffert, Jana Vranes, Jason Park, Jay Mahadeokar, Jeet Shah, Jelmer van der Linde, Jennifer Billock, Jenny Hong, Jenya Lee, Jeremy Fu, Jianfeng Chi, Jianyu Huang, Jiawen Liu, Jie Wang, Jiecao Yu, Joanna Bitton, Joe Spisak, Jongsoo Park, Joseph Rocca, Joshua Johnstun, Joshua Saxe, Junteng Jia, Kalyan Vasuden Alwala, Kartikeya Upasani, Kate Plawiak, Ke Li, Kenneth Heafield, Kevin Stone, Khalid El-Arini, Krithika Iyer, Kshitiz Malik, Kuenley Chiu, Kunal Bhalla, Lauren Rantala-Yeary, Laurens van der Maaten, Lawrence Chen, Liang Tan, Liz Jenkins, Louis Martin, Lovish Madaan, Lubo Malo, Lukas Blecher, Lukas Landzaat, Luke de Oliveira, Madeline Muzzi, Mahesh Pasupuleti, Mannat Singh, Manohar Paluri, Marcin Kardas, Mathew Oldham, Mathieu Rita, Maya Pavlova, Melanie Kambadur, Mike Lewis, Min Si, Mitesh Kumar Singh, Mona Hassan, Naman Goyal, Narjes Torabi, Nikolay Bashlykov, Nikolay Bogoychev, Niladri Chatterji, Olivier Duchenne, Onur Çelebi, Patrick Alrassy, Pengchuan Zhang, Pengwei Li, Petar Vasic, Peter Weng, Prajjwal Bhargava, Pratik Dubal, Praveen Krishnan, Punit Singh Koura, Puxin Xu, Qing He, Qingxiao Dong, Ragavan Srinivasan, Raj Ganapathy, Ramon Calderer, Ricardo Silveira Cabral, Robert Stojnic, Roberta Raileanu, Rohit Girdhar, Rohit Patel, Romain Sauvestre, Ronnie Polidoro, Roshan Sumbaly, Ross Taylor, Ruan Silva, Rui Hou, Rui Wang, Saghar Hosseini, Sahana Chennabasappa, Sanjay Singh, Sean Bell, Seohyun Sonia Kim, Sergey Edunov, Shaoliang Nie, Sharan Narang, Sharath Raparthy, Sheng Shen, Shengye Wan, Shruti Bhosale, Shun Zhang, Simon Vandenhende, Soumya Batra, Spencer Whitman, Sten Sootla, Stephane Collot, Suchin Gururangan, Sydney Borodinsky, Tamar Herman, Tara Fowler, Tarek Sheasha, Thomas Georgiou, Thomas Scialom, Tobias Speckbacher, Todor Mihaylov, Tong Xiao, Ujjwal Karn, Vedanuj Goswami, Vibhor Gupta, Vignesh Ramanathan, Viktor Kerkez, Vincent Gonguet, Virginie Do, Vish Vogeti, Vladan Petrovic, Weiwei Chu, Wenhan Xiong, Wenyin Fu, Whitney Meers, Xavier Martinet, Xiaodong Wang, Xiaoqing Ellen Tan, Xinfeng Xie, Xuchao Jia, Xuewei Wang, Yaelle Goldschlag, Yashesh Gaur, Yasmine Babaei, Yi Wen, Yiwen Song, Yuchen Zhang, Yue Li, Yuning Mao, Zacharie Delpierre Coudert, Zheng Yan, Zhengxing Chen, Zoe Papakipos, Aaditya Singh, Aaron Grattafiori, Abha Jain, Adam Kelsey, Adam Shajnfeld, Adithya Gangidi, Adolfo Victoria, Ahuva Goldstand, Ajay Menon, Ajay Sharma, Alex Boesenberg, Alex Vaughan, Alexei Baevski, Allie Feinstein, Amanda Kallet, Amit Sangani, Anam Yunus, Andrei Lupu, Andres Alvarado, Andrew Caples, Andrew Gu, Andrew Ho, Andrew Poulton, Andrew Ryan, Ankit Ramchandani, Annie Franco, Aparajita Saraf, Arkabandhu Chowdhury, Ashley Gabriel, Ashwin Bharambe, Assaf Eisenman, Azadeh Yazdan, Beau James, Ben Maurer, Benjamin Leonhardi, Bernie Huang, Beth Loyd, Beto De Paola, Bhargavi Paranjape, Bing Liu, Bo Wu, Boyu Ni, Braden Hancock, Bram Wasti, Brandon Spence, Brani Stojkovic, Brian Gamido, Britt Montalvo, Carl Parker, Carly Burton, Catalina Mejia, Changhan Wang, Changkyu Kim, Chao Zhou, Chester Hu, Ching-Hsiang Chu, Chris Cai, Chris Tindal, Christoph Feichtenhofer, Damon Civin, Dana Beaty, Daniel Kreymer, Daniel Li, Danny Wyatt, David Adkins, David Xu, Davide Testuggine, Delia David, Devi Parikh, Diana Liskovich, Didem Foss, Dingkang Wang, Duc Le, Dustin Holland, Edward Dowling, Eissa Jamil, Elaine Montgomery, Eleonora Presani, Emily Hahn, Emily Wood, Erik Brinkman, Esteban Arcaute, Evan Dunbar, Evan Smothers, Fei Sun, Felix Kreuk, Feng Tian, Firat Ozgenel, Francesco Caggioni, Francisco Guzmán, Frank Kanayet, Frank Seide, Gabriela Medina Florez, Gabriella Schwarz, Gada Badeer, Georgia Swee, Gil Halpern, Govind Thattai, Grant Herman, Grigory Sizov, Guangyi, Zhang, Guna Lakshminarayanan, Hamid Shojanazeri, Han Zou, Hannah Wang, Hanwen Zha, Haroun Habeeb, Harrison Rudolph, Helen Suk, Henry Aspegren, Hunter Goldman, Ibrahim Damlaj, Igor Molybog, Igor Tufanov, Irina-Elena Veliche, Itai Gat, Jake Weissman, James Geboski, James Kohli, Japhet Asher, Jean-Baptiste Gaya, Jeff Marcus, Jeff Tang, Jennifer Chan, Jenny Zhen, Jeremy Reizenstein, Jeremy Teboul, Jessica Zhong, Jian Jin, Jingyi Yang, Joe Cummings, Jon Carvill, Jon Shepard, Jonathan McPhie, Jonathan Torres, Josh Ginsburg, Junjie Wang, Kai Wu, Kam Hou U, Karan Saxena, Karthik Prasad, Kartikay Khandelwal, Katayoun Zand, Kathy Matosich, Kaushik Veeraraghavan, Kelly Michelena, Keqian Li, Kun Huang, Kunal Chawla, Kushal Lakhotia, Kyle Huang, Lailin Chen, Lakshya Garg, Lavender A, Leandro Silva, Lee Bell, Lei Zhang, Liangpeng Guo, Licheng Yu, Liron Moshkovich, Luca Wehrstedt, Madian Khabsa, Manav Avalani, Manish Bhatt, Maria Tsimpoukelli, Martynas Mankus, Matan Hasson, Matthew Lennie, Matthias Reso, Maxim Groshev, Maxim Naumov, Maya Lathi, Meghan Keneally, Michael L. Seltzer, Michal Valko, Michelle Restrepo, Mihir Patel, Mik Vyatskov, Mikayel Samvelyan, Mike Clark, Mike Macey, Mike Wang, Miquel Jubert Hermoso, Mo Metanat, Mohammad Rastegari, Munish Bansal, Nandhini Santhanam, Natascha Parks, Natasha White, Navyata Bawa, Nayan Singhal, Nick Egebo, Nicolas Usunier, Nikolay Pavlovich Laptev, Ning Dong, Ning Zhang, Norman Cheng, Oleg Chernoguz, Olivia Hart, Omkar Salpekar, Ozlem Kalinli, Parkin Kent, Parth Parekh, Paul Saab, Pavan Balaji, Pedro Rittner, Philip Bontrager, Pierre Roux, Piotr Dollar, Polina Zvyagina, Prashant Ratanchandani, Pritish Yuvraj, Qian Liang, Rachad Alao, Rachel Rodriguez, Rafi Ayub, Raghotham Murthy, Raghu Nayani, Rahul Mitra, Raymond Li, Rebekkah Hogan, Robin Battey, Rocky Wang, Rohan Maheswari, Russ Howes, Ruty Rinott, Sai Jayesh Bondu, Samyak Datta, Sara Chugh, Sara Hunt, Sargun Dhillon, Sasha Sidorov, Satadru Pan, Saurabh Verma, Seiji Yamamoto, Sharadh Ramaswamy, Shaun Lindsay, Shaun Lindsay, Sheng Feng, Shenghao Lin, Shengxin Cindy Zha, Shiva Shankar, Shuqiang Zhang, Shuqiang Zhang, Sinong Wang, Sneha Agarwal, Soji Sajuyigbe, Soumith Chintala, Stephanie Max, Stephen Chen, Steve Kehoe, Steve Satterfield, Sudarshan Govindaprasad, Sumit Gupta, Sungmin Cho, Sunny Virk, Suraj Subramanian, Sy Choudhury, Sydney Goldman, Tal Remez, Tamar Glaser, Tamara Best, Thilo Kohler, Thomas Robinson, Tianhe Li, Tianjun Zhang, Tim Matthews, Timothy Chou, Tzook Shaked, Varun Vontimitta, Victoria Ajayi, Victoria Montanez, Vijai Mohan, Vinay Satish Kumar, Vishal Mangla, Vítor Albiero, Vlad Ionescu, Vlad Poenaru, Vlad Tiberiu Mihailescu, Vladimir Ivanov, Wei Li, Wenchen Wang, Wenwen Jiang, Wes Bouaziz, Will Constable, Xiaocheng Tang, Xiaofang Wang, Xiaojian Wu, Xiaolan Wang, Xide Xia, Xilun Wu, Xinbo Gao, Yanjun Chen, Ye Hu, Ye Jia, Ye Qi, Yenda Li, Yilin Zhang, Ying Zhang, Yossi Adi, Youngjin Nam, Yu, Wang, Yuchen Hao, Yundi Qian, Yuzi He, Zach Rait, Zachary DeVito, Zef Rosnbrick, Zhaoduo Wen, Zhenyu Yang, and Zhiwei Zhao. 2024. The llama 3 herd of models.

Ariel Ekgren, Amaru Cuba Gyllensten, Felix Stollenwerk, Joey Öhman, Tim Isbister, Evangelia Gogoulou, Fredrik Carlsson, Alice Heiman, Judit Casademont, and Magnus Sahlgren. 2023. Gpt-sw3: An autoregressive language model for the nordic languages. *arXiv preprint arXiv:2305.12987*.

Naman Goyal, Cynthia Gao, Vishrav Chaudhary, Peng-Jen Chen, Guillaume Wenzek, Da Ju, Sanjana Krishnan, Marc'Aurelio Ranzato, Francisco Guzmán, and Angela Fan. 2022. The Flores-101 evaluation benchmark for low-resource and multilingual machine translation. *Transactions of the Association for Computational Linguistics*, 10:522–538.

Ashim Gupta and Vivek Srikumar. 2021. X-fact: A new benchmark dataset for multilingual fact checking. In *Proceedings of the 59th Annual Meeting of the Association for Computational Linguistics and the 11th International Joint Conference on Natural Language Processing (Volume 2: Short Papers)*, pages 675–682, Online. Association for Computational Linguistics.

Momchil Hardalov, Todor Mihaylov, Dimitrina Zlatkova, Yoan Dinkov, Ivan Koychev, and Preslav Nakov. 2020. EXAMS: A multi-subject high school examinations dataset for cross-lingual and multilingual question answering. In *Proceedings of the 2020 Conference on Empirical Methods in Natural Language Processing*, EMNLP '20, pages 5427–5444, Online. Association for Computational Linguistics.

Amr Hendy, Mohamed Abdelrehim, Amr Sharaf, Vikas Raunak, Mohamed Gabr, Hitokazu Matsushita, Young Jin Kim, Mohamed Afify, and Hany Hassan Awadalla. 2023. How good are gpt models at machine translation? a comprehensive evaluation. *arXiv preprint arXiv:2302.09210*.

Maxim Ifergan, Leshem Choshen, Roee Aharoni, Idan Szpektor, and Omri Abend. 2024. Beneath the surface of consistency: Exploring cross-lingual knowledge representation sharing in llms. *arXiv preprint arXiv:2408.10646*.

Gautier Izacard, Patrick Lewis, Maria Lomeli, Lucas Hosseini, Fabio Petroni, Timo Schick, Jane Dwivedi-Yu, Armand Joulin, Sebastian Riedel, and Edouard Grave. 2022. Few-shot Learning with Retrieval Augmented Language Models.

Albert Q. Jiang, Alexandre Sablayrolles, Arthur Mensch, Chris Bamford, Devendra Singh Chaplot, Diego de las Casas, Florian Bressand, Gianna Lengyel, Guillaume Lample, Lucile Saulnier, Lélio Renard Lavaud, Marie-Anne Lachaux, Pierre Stock, Teven Le Scao, Thibaut Lavril, Thomas Wang, Timothée Lacroix, and William El Sayed. 2023. Mistral 7b.

Wenxiang Jiao, Wenxuan Wang, Jen-tse Huang, Xing Wang, Shuming Shi, and Zhaopeng Tu. 2023. Is chatgpt a good translator? yes with gpt-4 as the engine. *arXiv preprint arXiv:2301.08745*.

Tom Kocmi, Eleftherios Avramidis, Rachel Bawden, Ondřej Bojar, Anton Dvorkovich, Christian Federmann, Mark Fishel, Markus Freitag, Thamme Gowda, Roman Grundkiewicz, Barry Haddow, Marzena Karpinska, Philipp Koehn, Benjamin Marie, Christof Monz, Kenton Murray, Masaaki Nagata, Martin Popel, Maja Popović, Mariya Shmatova, Steinthór Steingrímsson, and Vilém Zouhar. 2024. Findings of the WMT24 general machine translation shared task: The LLM era is here but MT is not solved yet. In *Proceedings of the Ninth Conference on Machine Translation*, pages 1–46, Miami, Florida, USA. Association for Computational Linguistics.

Tom Kocmi, Eleftherios Avramidis, Rachel Bawden, Ondřej Bojar, Anton Dvorkovich, Christian Federmann, Mark Fishel, Markus Freitag, Thamme Gowda, Roman Grundkiewicz, Barry Haddow, Philipp Koehn, Benjamin Marie, Christof Monz, Makoto Morishita, Kenton Murray, Makoto Nagata, Toshiaki Nakazawa, Martin Popel, Maja Popović, and Mariya Shmatova. 2023. Findings of the 2023 conference on machine translation (WMT23): LLMs are here but not quite there yet. In *Proceedings of the Eighth Conference on Machine Translation*, pages 1–42, Singapore. Association for Computational Linguistics.

Viet Lai, Chien Nguyen, Nghia Ngo, Thuat Nguyen, Franck Dernoncourt, Ryan Rossi, and Thien Nguyen. 2023. Okapi: Instruction-tuned large language models in multiple languages with reinforcement learning from human feedback. In *Proceedings of the 2023 Conference on Empirical Methods in Natural Language Processing: System Demonstrations*, pages 318–327, Singapore. Association for Computational Linguistics.

Li Linlin. 2024. Artificial intelligence translator deepl translation quality control. *Procedia Computer Science*, 247:710–717.

OpenAI, Josh Achiam, Steven Adler, Sandhini Agarwal, Lama Ahmad, Ilge Akkaya, Florencia Leoni Aleman, Diogo Almeida, Janko Altenschmidt, Sam Altman, Shyamal Anadkat, Red Avila, Igor Babuschkin, Suchir Balaji, Valerie Balcom, Paul Baltescu, Haiming Bao, Mohammad Bavarian, Jeff Belgum, Irwan Bello, Jake Berdine, Gabriel Bernadett-Shapiro, Christopher Berner, Lenny Bogdonoff, Oleg Boiko, Madelaine Boyd, Anna-Luisa Brakman, Greg Brockman, Tim Brooks, Miles Brundage, Kevin Button, Trevor Cai, Rosie Campbell, Andrew Cann, Brittany Carey, Chelsea Carlson, Rory Carmichael, Brooke Chan, Che Chang, Fotis Chantzis, Derek Chen, Sully Chen, Ruby Chen, Jason Chen, Mark Chen, Ben Chess, Chester Cho, Casey Chu, Hyung Won Chung, Dave Cummings, Jeremiah Currier, Yunxing Dai, Cory Decareaux, Thomas Degry, Noah Deutsch, Damien Deville, Arka Dhar, David Dohan, Steve Dowling, Sheila Dunning, Adrien Ecoffet, Atty Eleti, Tyna Eloundou, David Farhi, Liam Fedus, Niko Felix, Simón Posada Fishman, Juston Forte, Isabella Fulford, Leo Gao, Elie Georges, Christian Gibson, Vik Goel, Tarun Gogineni, Gabriel Goh, Rapha Gontijo-Lopes, Jonathan Gordon, Morgan Grafstein, Scott Gray, Ryan Greene, Joshua Gross, Shixiang Shane Gu, Yufei Guo, Chris Hallacy, Jesse Han, Jeff Harris, Yuchen He, Mike Heaton, Johannes Heidecke, Chris Hesse, Alan Hickey, Wade Hickey, Peter Hoeschele, Brandon Houghton, Kenny Hsu, Shengli Hu, Xin Hu, Joost Huizinga, Shantanu Jain, Shawn Jain, Joanne Jang, Angela Jiang, Roger Jiang, Haozhun Jin, Denny Jin, Shino Jomoto, Billie Jonn, Heewoo Jun, Tomer Kaftan, Łukasz Kaiser, Ali Kamali, Ingmar Kanitscheider, Nitish Shirish Keskar, Tabarak Khan, Logan Kilpatrick, Jong Wook Kim, Christina Kim, Yongjik Kim, Jan Hendrik Kirchner, Jamie Kiros, Matt Knight, Daniel Kokotajlo, Łukasz Kondraciuk, Andrew Kondrich, Aris Konstantinidis, Kyle Kosic, Gretchen Krueger, Vishal Kuo, Michael Lampe, Ikai Lan, Teddy Lee, Jan Leike, Jade Leung, Daniel Levy, Chak Ming Li, Rachel Lim, Molly Lin, Stephanie Lin, Mateusz Litwin, Theresa Lopez, Ryan Lowe, Patricia Lue, Anna Makanju, Kim Malfacini, Sam Manning, Todor Markov, Yaniv Markovski, Bianca Martin, Katie Mayer, Andrew Mayne, Bob McGrew, Scott Mayer McKinney, Christine McLeavey, Paul McMillan, Jake McNeil, David Medina, Aalok Mehta, Jacob Menick, Luke Metz, Andrey Mishchenko, Pamela Mishkin, Vinnie Monaco, Evan Morikawa, Daniel Mossing, Tong Mu, Mira Murati, Oleg Murk, David Mély, Ashvin Nair, Reiichiro Nakano, Rajeev Nayak, Arvind Neelakantan, Richard Ngo, Hyeonwoo Noh, Long Ouyang, Cullen O'Keefe, Jakub Pachocki, Alex Paino, Joe Palermo, Ashley Pantuliano, Giambattista Parascandolo, Joel Parish, Emy Parparita, Alex Passos, Mikhail Pavlov, Andrew Peng, Adam Perelman, Filipe de Avila Belbute Peres, Michael Petrov, Henrique Ponde de Oliveira Pinto, Michael, Pokorny, Michelle Pokrass, Vitchyr H. Pong, Tolly Powell, Alethea Power, Boris Power, Elizabeth Proehl, Raul Puri, Alec Radford, Jack Rae, Aditya Ramesh, Cameron Raymond, Francis Real, Kendra Rimbach, Carl Ross, Bob Rotsted, Henri Roussez, Nick Ryder, Mario Saltarelli, Ted Sanders, Shibani Santurkar, Girish Sastry, Heather Schmidt, David Schnurr, John Schulman, Daniel Selsam, Kyla Sheppard, Toki Sherbakov, Jessica Shieh, Sarah Shoker, Pranav Shyam, Szymon Sidor, Eric Sigler, Maddie Simens, Jordan Sitkin, Katarina Slama, Ian Sohl, Benjamin Sokolowsky, Yang Song, Natalie Staudacher, Felipe Petroski Such, Natalie Summers, Ilya Sutskever, Jie Tang, Nikolas Tezak, Madeleine B. Thompson, Phil Tillet, Amin Tootoonchian, Elizabeth Tseng, Preston Tuggle, Nick Turley, Jerry Tworek, Juan Felipe Cerón Uribe, Andrea Vallone, Arun Vijayvergiya, Chelsea Voss, Carroll Wainwright, Justin Jay Wang, Alvin Wang, Ben Wang, Jonathan Ward, Jason Wei, CJ Weinmann, Akila Welihinda, Peter Welinder, Jiayi Weng, Lilian Weng, Matt Wiethoff, Dave Willner, Clemens Winter, Samuel Wolrich, Hannah Wong, Lauren Workman, Sherwin Wu, Jeff Wu, Michael Wu, Kai Xiao, Tao Xu, Sarah Yoo, Kevin Yu, Qiming Yuan, Wojciech Zaremba, Rowan Zellers, Chong Zhang, Marvin Zhang, Shengjia Zhao, Tianhao Zheng, Juntang Zhuang, William Zhuk, and Barret Zoph. 2024. Gpt-4 technical report.

Jirui Qi, Raquel Fernández, and Arianna Bisazza. 2023. Cross-lingual consistency of factual knowledge in multilingual language models. *arXiv preprint arXiv:2310.10378*.

Rajesh Ranjan, Shailja Gupta, and Surya Narayan Singh. 2024. A comprehensive survey of bias in llms: Current landscape and future directions.

Shahnewaz Karim Sakib and Anindya Bijoy Das. 2024. Unveiling and mitigating bias in large language model recommendations: A path to fairness.

Qwen Team. 2024. Qwen2.5: A party of foundation models.

Klaudia Thellmann, Bernhard Stadler, Michael Fromm, Jasper Schulze Buschhoff, Alex Jude, Fabio Barth, Johannes Leveling, Nicolas Flores-Herr, Joachim Köhler, René Jäkel, et al. 2024. Towards multilingual llm evaluation for european languages. *arXiv preprint arXiv:2410.08928*.

Jiaan Wang, Yunlong Liang, Zengkui Sun, Yuxuan Cao, Jiarong Xu, and Fandong Meng. 2023. Cross-lingual knowledge editing in large language models. *arXiv preprint arXiv:2309.08952*.

Jingjing Wang. 2024. Exploring the potential of chatgpt-4o in translation quality assessment. *Journal of Theory and Practice in Humanities and Social Sciences*, 1(3):18–30.

Thomas Wolf, Lysandre Debut, Victor Sanh, Julien Chaumond, Clement Delangue, Anthony Moi, Pierric Cistac, Tim Rault, Rémi Louf, Morgan Funtowicz, Joe Davison, Sam Shleifer, Patrick von Platen, Clara Ma, Yacine Jernite, Julien Plu, Canwen Xu, Teven Le Scao, Sylvain Gugger, Mariama Drame, Quentin Lhoest, and Alexander M. Rush. 2020. Transformers: State-of-the-art natural language processing. In *Proceedings of the 2020 Conference on Empirical Methods in Natural Language Processing: System Demonstrations*, pages 38–45, Online. Association for Computational Linguistics.

An Yang, Baosong Yang, Binyuan Hui, Bo Zheng, Bowen Yu, Chang Zhou, Chengpeng Li, Chengyuan Li, Dayiheng Liu, Fei Huang, Guanting Dong, Haoran Wei, Huan Lin, Jialong Tang, Jialin Wang, Jian Yang, Jianhong Tu, Jianwei Zhang, Jianxin Ma, Jin Xu, Jingren Zhou, Jinze Bai, Jinzheng He, Junyang Lin, Kai Dang, Keming Lu, Keqin Chen, Kexin Yang, Mei Li, Mingfeng Xue, Na Ni, Pei Zhang, Peng Wang, Ru Peng, Rui Men, Ruize Gao, Runji Lin, Shijie Wang, Shuai Bai, Sinan Tan, Tianhang Zhu, Tianhao Li, Tianyu Liu, Wenbin Ge, Xiaodong Deng, Xiaohuan Zhou, Xingzhang Ren, Xinyu Zhang, Xipin Wei, Xuancheng Ren, Yang Fan, Yang Yao, Yichang Zhang, Yu Wan, Yunfei Chu, Yuqiong Liu, Zeyu Cui, Zhenru Zhang, and Zhihao Fan. 2024. Qwen2 technical report. *arXiv preprint arXiv:2407.10671*.

Yinfei Yang, Yuan Zhang, Chris Tar, and Jason Baldridge. 2019. PAWS-X: A cross-lingual adversarial dataset for paraphrase identification. In *Proceedings of the 2019 Conference on Empirical Methods in Natural Language Processing and the 9th International Joint Conference on Natural Language Processing (EMNLP-IJCNLP)*, pages 3687–3692, Hong Kong, China. Association for Computational Linguistics.

Xin Zhao, Naoki Yoshinaga, and Daisuke Oba. 2024. Tracing the roots of facts in multilingual language models: Independent, shared, and transferred knowledge. *arXiv preprint arXiv:2403.05189*.

Wenhao Zhu, Hongyi Liu, Qingxiu Dong, Jingjing Xu, Lingpeng Kong, Jiajun Chen, Lei Li, and Shujian Huang. 2023. Multilingual machine translation with large language models: Empirical results and analysis. *ArXiv*, abs/2304.04675.

A Manual Translation Quality Evaluation

The annotation guidelines and examples can be found in our GitHub repository. For each translated language, we utilized the same following strategy. We recruited native speaker annotators, who are also are proficient in English. They were presented with 80 random samples from the dataset distinct for each annotator and 20 samples that are the same for each annotator. From those 80 samples, 40 were selected from a pool of Lithuanian history questions, and other 40 from the general history question. The same approach was applied for the remaining 20 samples: 10 were selected from a pool of Lithuanian history questions, and other 10 from the general history question.

The annotators were presented with the translated English question, its answer choices and the corresponding translation for the question and choices. in the case of Lithuanian to English translation, the pairs of Lithuanian and English were presented. They were instructed to determine if the translation is correct from the following standpoints. The translation accurately conveys the meaning of the English or Lithuanian text. The

Lang Pair	# Reject (A)	# Reject (B)	# Accept (A)	# Accept (B)	Intersect, %	Cohen Kappa
LT-EN	11	18	89	82	75	0.286
EN-UA	10	30	90	70	75	0.286
EN-AR	28	21	72	79	65	0.239
LT-EST*	13	54	87	46	0.55	0.0
EN-SW	1	6	99	94	0.9	-0.053
EN-DN	9	41	91	59	0.6	-0.013
EN-FN	15	33	78	67	0.73	0.189
LT-LAV*	27	43	73	57	0.7	0.381

Table 3: Annotation results. * indicates translation with DeepL from Lithuanian to the target language. # Reject and Accept refer to a number of rejected and accepted samples by the annotator (marked with letters A and B). Intersect indicates a percentage of samples that annotators assigned the same label.

order of answers (with respect to the letters) is the same in both languages. The names of historical figures, locations, dates, or events are correctly translated and align with conventions. Text semantics are clear and do not change the intent or emphasis of the question or answers. If the translation contains grammar or phrasing issues, or minor typos, they do not lead to confusion or ambiguity and do not change the semantics.

If the translation does not fit the requirements above, the translation is rejected. The annotation results and agreements (in a form of number of intersections and Cohen Kappa scores) are presented in the Table 3. During our experiments, chatGPT showed poor results when translating to Latvian and Estonian. Therefore, we used DeepL to translated Lithuanian to Latvian and Estonian. The annotation in the Table 3 corresponds to DeepL translation.

The obtained Cohen Kappa scores were not high, especially for Swedish and Danish. As we only had 20 samples for comparison (Bujang and Baharum, 2017), the Cohen Kappa score is not reliable in this case, we additionally calculated the number of intersections.

Evaluating LLM Judgment on Latvian and Lithuanian Short Answer Matching

Yevhen Kostiuk[1,2]
[1]ARG-tech,
University of Dundee
[2]OpenBabylon
ykostiuk001@dundee.ac.uk

Oxana Vitman
University of Bremen

Łukasz Gagała
Georg-August
Universität Göttingen

Artur Kiulian
OpenBabylon

Abstract

In this work, we address the challenge of evaluating large language models (LLMs) on the short answer matching task for Latvian and Lithuanian languages. We introduce novel datasets consisting of 502 Latvian and 690 Lithuanian question-answer pairs. For each question-answer pair, we generated matched and non-matched answers using a set of alteration rules specifically designed to introduce small but meaningful changes in the text. These generated answers serve as test cases to assess the ability of LLMs to detect subtle differences in matching of the original answers. A subset of the datasets was manually verified for quality and accuracy. Our results show that while larger LLMs, such as QWEN2.5 72b and LLaMa3.1 70b, demonstrate near-perfect performance in distinguishing matched and non-matched answers, smaller models show more variance. For instance, LLaMa3.1 8b and EuroLLM 9b benefited from few-shot examples, while Mistral Nemo 12b underperformed on detection of subtle text alteration, particularly in Lithuanian, even with additional examples. QWEN2.5 7b and Mistral 7b were able to obtain a strong and comparable performance to the larger 70b models in zero and few shot experiments. Moreover, the performance of Mistral 7b was weaker in few shot experiments. The code and the dataset are available on our GitHub[1].

1 Introduction

In educational domain, open-ended questions are commonly used and can be defined as questions that require a more elaborate response than simple yes-no or selection of a correct choice. These questions help to encourage a discussion, share ideas and provide more freedom for a student.

Evaluation of responses to the open-ended question is a time-consuming and difficult task that requires an evaluator to carefully read each answer and compare it with the correct answers, ensuring they match. Automating this process makes it easier for evaluators to provide a feedback and analyze errors faster (Pillai et al., 2018; Sreevidhya and Narayanan, 2021).

The automatic short answer matching task addresses this challenge. The goal of the task is to predict whether an answer to the question is matching a correct answer. With the introduction of LLMs, reasonable performance was achieved on English and other high-resource languages for this problem (Ivanova and Handschuh, 2024). On the other hand, when it comes to low-resource settings, LLMs demonstrated weaker results, as well as displayed biases (Hackl et al., 2023; Lai et al., 2023).

In this work, we focus on Latvian and Lithuanian answer matching task, specifically on a detection of correct and incorrect responses that are similar to a set of reference "gold" answers, but differ in the key detail(s) to the question.

We automatically generated open-ended question-answer datasets for these languages based on Wikipedia. For this task, we do not focus on the factual correctness of the answers. Each element of the dataset contains a question and its reference answer. Then we generated a set of answers that are matched with the reference answer and a set of non-matched answers. The non-matched answers are created as similarly as possible to the reference answers with respect to the words inclusion, but with the key words changed to make it incorrect. To generate the answers, we formulated different text *alteration*

[1]https://github.com/OpenBabylon/NoDaLiDa2025-Latvian-Lithuanian-SAM

Proceedings of the 1st NB-REAL Workshop 2025 - Nordic-Baltic Responsible Evaluation and Alignment of Language models, pages 12–41
March 2, 2025

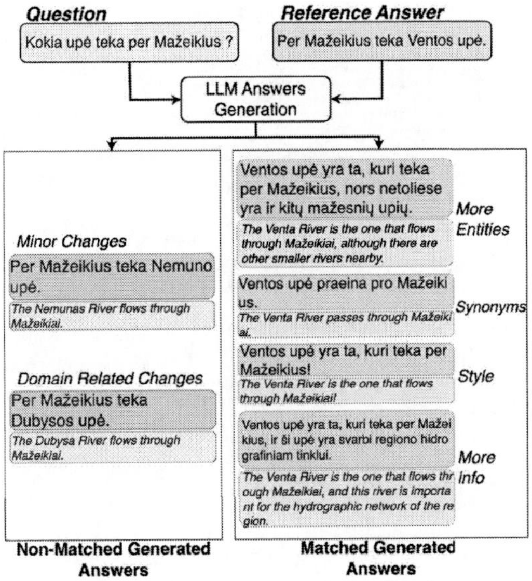

Figure 1: Example of the element from Lithuanian generated dataset.

rules (**AR**) that are minor when it comes to a text change, but semantically are major. For each rule, the different LLMs with a few shot generation process were used. Finally, to ensure the quality, we manually evaluated a sample of the data and filtered the final dataset based on it. We expect the models to obtain high, almost perfect, results on this task.

We formulated the following research questions in this paper.

Q1: Are LLMs capable of correctly identifying matched and non-matched answers with the proposed alteration rules?

Q2: Is there a difference between few-shot and zero-shot inference for different LLMs for this task?

Our contributions are the following:

- We automatically generated a dataset of 502 Latvian and 690 Lithuanian question-answer pairs based on Wikipedia. We defined and generated a list of matched and non-matched answers to each pair of question-answer, resulting in 3,012 and 4,830 elements for Latvian and Lithuanian respectively, and partially manually evaluated samples of the datasets.
- We evaluated LLaMa3.1 (8b and 70b) (Dubey et al., 2024), Mistral Nemo 12b and Mistral 7b (Jiang et al., 2023), EuroLLM 9b (Martins et al., 2024), and QWEN2.5 (7b and 72b) (Team, 2024; Yang et al., 2024) models and compared their achieved accuracy scores per AR and overall.
- We evaluated the models in zero-shot and few-shot settings and their performance based on different ARs of matched and non-matched answers.

Our findings showed that larger LLMs, such as QWEN2.5 72b and LLaMa3.1 70b, consistently performed well across both Latvian and Lithuanian datasets, effectively distinguishing matched and non-matched answers in both zero shot and few shot experiments. However, smaller models demonstrated variation in their results. LLaMa3.1 8b and EuroLLM 9b showed improved performance with few-shot examples, while Mistral Nemo 12b showed limitations, particularly in Lithuanian. QWEN2.5 7b and Mistral 7b were able to obtain a similar performance to the larger 70b models, with Mistral 7b showing weaker performance in few shot experiments.

2 Related Work

Answer matching task can be viewed as a subtask of the automatic short answer grading (ASAG). The definition of what is a short answer and if it is acceptable can vary depending on the domain (Burrows et al., 2015; Bonthu et al., 2021). Nevertheless, all the definitions involve high semantic similarity between the correct answer(s) and predicted answers. The grading scale is also can be domain dependent (Zhang et al.; Divya et al., 2023; Krithika and Narayanan, 2015).

With the development of deep learning methods, they were widely used for the task, as they provide better robustness towards syntactic changes of the text rather than other methods (Bonthu et al., 2021), utilizing RNNs (Cai, 2019), CNNs (Chen and Zhou, 2019), transformers (Sung et al., 2019; Willms and Padó, 2022) and so on. Some of the suggested methods are aimed to not only grade an answer, but to explain its flows and inaccuracies (Tornqvist et al., 2023).

With the rise of generative large language models (LLMs), they were applied for ASAG as well (Metzler et al., 2024; Ivanova and Handschuh, 2024; Chu et al., 2024; Schneider et al., 2023; Grévisse, 2024; Yancey et al., 2023; Yoon,

2023). Analysis of LLMs for this task showed that they are capable of predicting consistent ratings for English (Hackl et al., 2023; Mizumoto and Eguchi, 2023). However, studies showed that the LLMs' performance on the non-English datasets is weaker (Lai et al., 2023; Darģis et al., 2024).

On the other hand, as any other NLP task, there is a gap in the ASAG resources for low-resource languages, including Nordic and Baltic. This area lacks high-quality datasets for these languages. The GPT-3.5 and GPT-4 models were evaluated on Finnish ASAG (Chang and Ginter, 2024) on the dataset of students' answers in Finnish for multiple subjects. The study demonstrated that the models assigned higher scores to the students' answers than the human annotator and achieving Quadratic Weighted Kappa (QWK) score of 0.44. In (Chang et al., 2022), the authors considered ASAG task as a paraphrase retrieval task, evaluating classical methods (TF-IDF) and different transformer methods.

In (Darģis et al., 2022), the self-assessment platform for Latvian language learners was proposed and developed. The authors generated exercises automatically based on data from multiple corpora (Levāne-Petrova et al., 2023; Darģis et al., 2022). In (Stefanovič et al., 2024), the research on detecting AI generated answers in Lithuanian was conducted, producing a dataset with student answers, GPT generated answers and its paraphrased versions. The authors (Weegar and Idestam-Almquist, 2024) created a dataset of student answers in Swedish in programming languages, networking and the Internet, and data abstractions and manipulations. The authors examined different machine learning methods to tackle the task. In (Klevstuen, 2022), the use of information retrieval and text mining methods were investigated to evaluate the content of Norwegian exam answers in Computer Science. In our work, we release multi-domain publicly available datasets as well as benchmark results for some of the open-source multilingual LLMs.

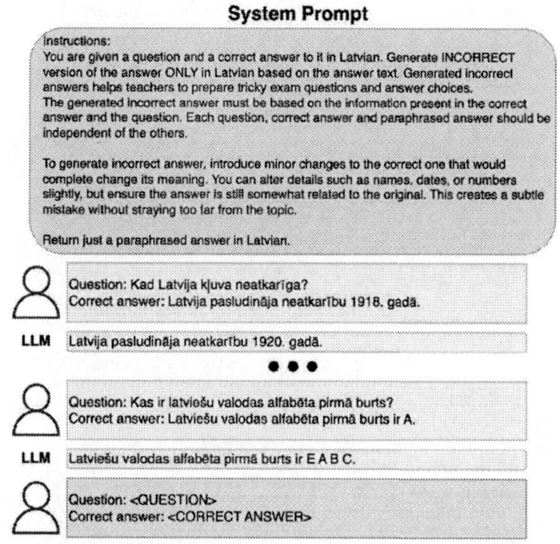

Figure 2: Example of few-shot incorporating minor changes prompt for non-matched answers generation in Latvian. $< \ldots >$ indicate the sample that requires prediction.

3 Datasets

To generate answer matching datasets, the three-stage pipeline was implemented.

Firstly, we used the approach for generating question-answer Knowledge and Instruction Dataset (KID) based on Wikipedia, introduced in (Kiulian et al., 2024) and adapted it for Latvian (Lat-KID) and Lithuanian (Lit-KID). More details are provided in the Section 3.1. The generated datasets consist of pairs of a question and a reference answer (assumed to be correct and relevant to the question), as well as a factual information that supports the answer.

In the second stage, for each pair of question and answer, we defined a list of different *alteration rules* that rewrites reference answer to matched or non-matched (more details are provided in the Section 3.2). We used GPT-4o and LLaMa3 8b (see Figure 1), utilizing separate prompts for each rule. The non-matched prompts were composed in a way that preserves as much words and semantics of the reference answer as possible with changing key words of the answer, while matched prompts are more flexible.

Finally, the generated results were validated and methods were filtered based on the accept ratio (more details are provided in the Section 3.3). A limitation of the approach it that we used LLMs for the benchmark generation, which could introduce an additional bias to the final dataset.

3.1 Lat-KID and Lit-KID Question-Answering Datasets

For each language, we extracted the top 1,000 articles for each month of the last 12 month from Wikipedia, resulting in 12,000 articles. From this pool, 1,000 articles with the top cumulative counts were extracted. The articles were filtered by their relevance to the corresponding country with Gemini 1.5 Pro (Team et al., 2024). Each article was separated into paragraphs and at least 3 questions were generated for it with Gemini 1.5 Pro. The prompt contains additional fields to run a self-check on the quality of the question (standalone, in the correct language, natural sounding). The prompts are available in the project's GitHub.

The obtained Lat-KID dataset has 502 unique questions. The average number of words in the question is 9.83 and in the answer is 24.37. The total number of words in the dataset (questions and reference answers) is 17,172. The unique amount of words is 5,058.

The obtained Lit-KID dataset has 690 unique questions. The average number of words in the question is 9.88 and in the answer is 29.02. The total number of words in the dataset (questions and reference answers) is 26,849. The unique amount of words is 7,725.

3.2 Matched and Non-Matched Answers Generation

Non-Matched Answers Generation. We defined two alteration rules for non-matched answers generation: incorporating minor changes (**IMC**) and changing domain related information (**CDRI**). IMC includes changes to the text that change a couple of key words like date, name, location etc, while keeping everything else unchanged. CDRI is similar to IMC, however its objective is to change a key term to the similar from the same domain. For example, changing the name of the first president to the second one, changing the word "Parliament" to "President" etc. With the **CDRI** method, the model is prompted to generated something that seems correct and from the same domain, but it is not.

To generate non-matched answers, we utilized LLaMa3 7b[2] and GPT-4o[3]. We selected these models for benchmark creation based on their performance and multilingual capabilities (Darģis et al., 2024).

When generating IMC and CDRI answers, the model was presented with the few-shot example prompts (see Figure 2).

[2]After manual evaluation, only IMC were generation was accepted for Lat-KID and CDRI for Lit-KID.

[3]We experimented with LLaMa2 13b, however manual evaluation showed much worse results.

Matched Answers Generation. We defined the following alteration rules for matched answers generation: adding more question-related entities (**Ents**), changing words to synonyms (**Synonyms**), adding more background information (**MoreInfo**), and style swap to exclamatory (**Exclamatory**).

As previously, we used GPT-4o and LLaMa3 7b. The models were presented with different prompts per rule. The code and prompts are available in the project's GitHub repository .

Postprocessing. After generating the answers, the duplicates were removed. The resulting amount of (question, reference answer, generated answer) triplets is 3,012 (1,506 are matched and other 1,506 are non-matched) for Latvian and 4,830 (2,760 are matched and 2,070 are non-matched) for Lithuanian. The amount of matched answers is 3,697. The amount of non-matched answers is 1,809.

3.3 Manual Evaluation

We recruited two native speakers for Latvian and Lithuanian to evaluate the quality of the final generated dataset. They were presented with a random triplet of (question, reference answer, generated answer) and a description if the generated answer was generated by matched or non-matched method. Based on that, the annotators had to accept a triplet if the description fits the reference and generated answers. Otherwise, they had to reject sample. The results are presented in Appendix A. The examples of rejected samples are presented in the Appendix B.

4 Methodology

To evaluate the LLMs capabilities and an influence of the prompting strategy, we used two prompting methods per language for this task: zero shot (**ZS**) and few shot (**FS**). We set all the parameters to defaults with a random seed of 2.

In all of the methods, the models were instructed to start their output with *True* if the provided reference answer and a generated answer are matched otherwise with *False*. ZS and FS shared the same system prompt, but FS gave a model additional examples in corresponding language.

We evaluated LLaMa3.1 (8b and 70b) (Dubey et al., 2024), Mistral Nemo 12b and Mistral 7b (Jiang et al., 2023), and QWEN2.5 (7b and 72b) (Team, 2024; Yang et al., 2024) models. To

	LT		LV	
	ZS	FS	ZS	FS
QWEN2.5;72b	0	1	0	0
LLaMa3.1:70b	1	8	1	3
Mistral:12b	0	1	0	0
EuroLLM:9b	0	0	2,845	4
LLaMa3.1:8b	111	30	2	10
QWEN2.5:7b	0	4	0	2
Mistral:7b	0	0	0	0

Table 1: Number of samples, where the model failed to produce an acceptable (parsable) answer.

	LT		*LV*	
	ZS	FS	ZS	FS
QWEN2.5 72b	0.99	0.99	0.99	0.99
LLaMa3.1 70b	0.99	0.99	0.99	0.99
Mistral Nemo 12b	0.96	0.94	0.96	0.94
EuroLLM 9b	0.13	0.97	0.05	0.84
LLaMa3.1 8b	0.89	0.98	0.87	0.96
QWEN2.5 7b	0.98	0.98	0.97	0.97
Mistral 7b	0.95	0.91	0.95	0.91

Table 2: F1 scores of binary matching. *LT* and *LV* refer to Lithuanian and Latvian respectively. ZS and FS refer to zero shot and few shot respectively.

parse the output, we checked if the model followed instructions about the output. If it did not, we retrieved the key words: "True" or "False". If none of the words were presented, we counted it as an incorrect prediction (see Table 1).

5 Results and Discussion

The results are presented in Table 2, and on Figures 3 and 4. Additionally, we measured the percentage of times, when model followed the provided format and started with "True" or "False". The majority of models were able to output the correct format for 99% on Latvian samples. For Lithuanian, LLaMa3.1 8b generated text in correct format in 89% of times in ZS settings. In case of the FS, this value is 99%. Other models consistently followed the format with a rate of 99%. EuroLLM 9b was not able to follow a format at all in ZS settings for both languages, even though its results were legible, but impossible to parse. However, when presented with a few shot examples, it generated expected format.

Our results demonstrated that larger LLMs (with 70b parameters) are capable of reliably detect matched and non-matched answers in Lithuanian and Latvian. We hypothesized that LLMs would output near perfect scores, however, smaller models performed differently. In the case of Mistral Nemo, there was a slight decrease of results when switched from zero shot to a few shot approach in both languages. On the contrary, LLaMa3.1 8b performed better in a few shot scenario, improving its ZS score on 9%. QWEN2.5 7b performed nearly perfectly, achieving 99 accuracy score in both settings.

Deeper analysis of results indicated that in case of Latvian, most of the models (except for LLaMa3.1 8b, MIstral 7b, and EuroLLM 9b) showed almost perfect performance on all the generated types of matched and non-matched answers. LLaMa3.1 8b was able to pick up non-matched answers in ZS and FS settings, but struggled with matched answers, demonstrating a bias towards negative answers. However, exposing it with the additional examples boosted its scores to the same level as others. EuroLLM was not able to follow instructions in zero shot prompts, therefore performing poorly. However, in the few shot settings, the model was able to detect non-matched answers, but had less success with matching answers, demonstrating bias towards negative answers. Mistral 7b perfromed well in ZS experiments, but showed a weaker performance in FS for non-match generated samples.

For Lithuanian, the least reliable model was Mistral Nemo 12b. It demonstrated a strong performance on the matched answers with more information and more entities, but was not able to effectively detect synonyms changes in both ZS and FS settings. In case of this model, providing more examples to the model did not have a noticeable effect. Interestingly, EuroLLM showed the same pattern as for Latvian in ZS, but was able to get a comparable results with the 70b groups of models in FS settings. It indicates that the model has a better understanding of Lithuanian than Latvian when it comes to this task, and can perform well when provided with examples.

Therefore, based on our observations, we can address each of the research questions we formulated.

Q1: Are LLMs capable of correctly identifying matched and non-matched answers with the proposed alteration rules ? Overall, the evaluated models were able to accurately identify, which

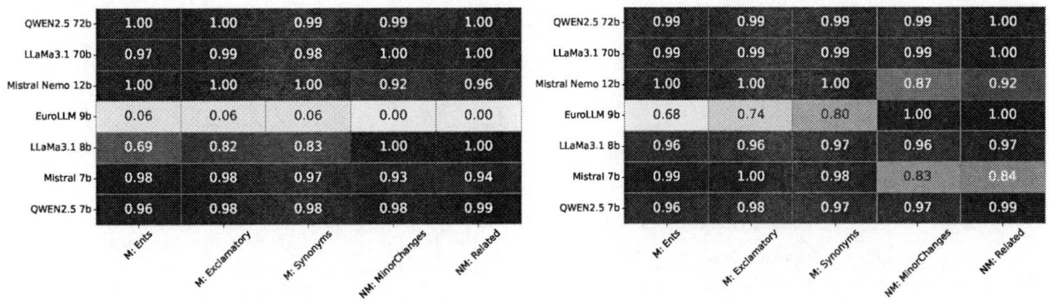

(a) Zero shot (b) Few shot

Figure 3: Accuracy scores per generated answer type for Latvian.

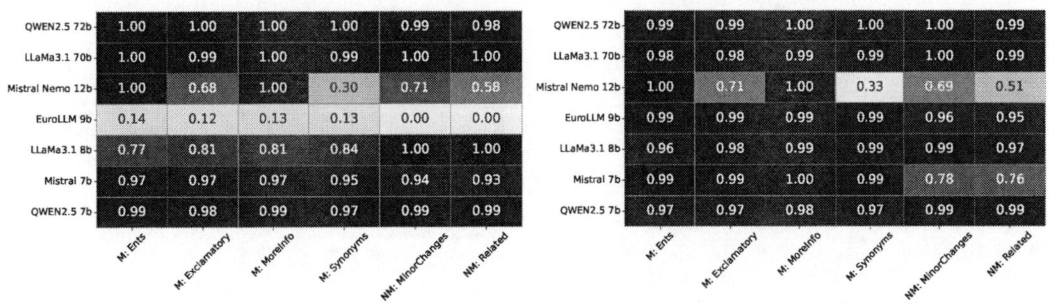

(a) Zero shot (b) Few shot

Figure 4: Accuracy scores per generated answer type for Lithuanian.

answers are matched and which are not. LLMs with the greater number of parameters showed a very consistent performance, when smaller model can have difficulties with Latvian or Lithuanian. Specifically, LLaMa3.1 8b and EuroLLM 9b require additional examples, when QWEN2.5 7b and Mistral 7b are on par with the larger models. Moreover, we found specific types of alternation rules that models had more difficulties to pick up. Specifically LLaMa3.1 8b and EuroLLM 9b had difficulties with added entities in the text in Latvian. Mistral 7b struggled with incorporating minor changes and changing domain related information rules in Latvian FS settings. Mistral Nemo obtained weaker performance on changing words to synonyms and style swap to exclamatory (**Exclamatory**) rules in Lithuanian.

Q2: Is there a difference between few-shot and zero-shot inference for different LLMs for this task ? Our findings showed that few shot approach did not improve the scores of the larger models: they are already very high. However, it can be helpful in case of some smaller models, especially with EuroLLM 9b. In case of Mistral 7b, the perfromance was decreased with adding more examples. On the other hand, if the model struggles with a language, providing more examples will not necessarily improves its performance (e.g. Mistral Nemo in Lithuanian or Mistral 7b) for this task.

6 Conclusion

In conclusion, our findings demonstrate that large language models (LLMs) with greater parameter counts, such as QWEN2.5 72b and LLaMa3.1 70b, consistently achieve high accuracy in distinguishing matched and non-matched answers across both Latvian and Lithuanian, regardless of zero-shot or few-shot settings. Smaller models showed less robustness, with LLaMa3.1 8b and EuroLLM 9b benefiting from additional examples in few-shot scenarios. Mistral Nemo 12b struggled with detecting certain nuances, particularly in Lithuanian. QWEN2.5 7b and Mistral 7b were able to obtain a similar the performance to the larger 70b models, but in case of Mistral 7b the performance decreased in with a few shot approach. These results highlight the robustness of larger models and the potential for targeted improvements in smaller ones to address answer matching task with the defined set of alteration rules.

Acknowledgments

This chapter is a product of the research conducted in the Collaborative Research Center 1342 "Global Dynamics of Social Policy". The center is funded by the Deutsche Forschungsgemeinschaft (DFG, German Research Foundation)—project number 374666841—SFB 1342. We would like to express our gratitude to the following organizations for their generous support, which made this work possible: GCP (Google Cloud) for providing credits used for model training and inference, and Tensorwave for providing AMD MI300X instance for inference and evaluations.

References

Sridevi Bonthu, S Rama Sree, and MHM Krishna Prasad. 2021. Automated short answer grading using deep learning: A survey. In *Machine Learning and Knowledge Extraction: 5th IFIP TC 5, TC 12, WG 8.4, WG 8.9, WG 12.9 International Cross-Domain Conference, CD-MAKE 2021, Virtual Event, August 17–20, 2021, Proceedings 5*, pages 61–78. Springer.

Steven Burrows, Iryna Gurevych, and Benno Stein. 2015. The eras and trends of automatic short answer grading. *International journal of artificial intelligence in education*, 25:60–117.

Changzhi Cai. 2019. Automatic essay scoring with recurrent neural network. In *Proceedings of the 3rd International Conference on High Performance Compilation, Computing and Communications*, pages 1–7.

Li-Hsin Chang and Filip Ginter. 2024. Automatic short answer grading for finnish with chatgpt. In *Proceedings of the AAAI Conference on Artificial Intelligence*, volume 38, pages 23173–23181.

Li-Hsin Chang, Jenna Kanerva, and Filip Ginter. 2022. Towards automatic short answer assessment for Finnish as a paraphrase retrieval task. In *Proceedings of the 17th Workshop on Innovative Use of NLP for Building Educational Applications (BEA 2022)*, pages 262–271, Seattle, Washington. Association for Computational Linguistics.

Zhiyun Chen and Yuxin Zhou. 2019. Research on automatic essay scoring of composition based on cnn and or. In *2019 2nd International Conference on Artificial Intelligence and Big Data (ICAIBD)*, pages 13–18. IEEE.

Yucheng Chu, Hang Li, Kaiqi Yang, Harry Shomer, Hui Liu, Yasemin Copur-Gencturk, and Jiliang Tang. 2024. A llm-powered automatic grading framework with human-level guidelines optimization. *arXiv preprint arXiv:2410.02165*.

Jacob Cohen. 1960. A coefficient of agreement for nominal scales. *Educational and psychological measurement*, 20(1):37–46.

Roberts Darģis, Ilze Auziņa, Inga Kaija, Kristīne Levāne-Petrova, and Kristīne Pokratniece. 2022. Corpus based self-assessment platform for latvian language learners. *Baltic Journal of Modern Computing*.

Roberts Darģis, Ilze Auziņa, Inga Kaija, Kristīne Levāne-Petrova, and Kristīne Pokratniece. 2022. LaVA – Latvian language learner corpus. In *Proceedings of the Thirteenth Language Resources and Evaluation Conference*, pages 727–731, Marseille, France. European Language Resources Association.

Roberts Darģis, Guntis Bārzdiņš, Inguna Skadiņa, and Baiba Saulite. 2024. Evaluating open-source LLMs in low-resource languages: Insights from Latvian high school exams. In *Proceedings of the 4th International Conference on Natural Language Processing for Digital Humanities*, pages 289–293, Miami, USA. Association for Computational Linguistics.

Arunima Divya, Vivek Haridas, and Jayasree Narayanan. 2023. Automation of short answer grading techniques: Comparative study using deep learning techniques. In *2023 Fifth International Conference on Electrical, Computer and Communication Technologies (ICECCT)*, pages 1–7. IEEE.

Abhimanyu Dubey, Abhinav Jauhri, Abhinav Pandey, Abhishek Kadian, Ahmad Al-Dahle, Aiesha Letman, Akhil Mathur, Alan Schelten, Amy Yang, Angela Fan, Anirudh Goyal, Anthony Hartshorn, Aobo Yang, Archi Mitra, Archie Sravankumar, Artem Korenev, Arthur Hinsvark, Arun Rao, Aston Zhang, Aurelien Rodriguez, Austen Gregerson, Ava Spataru, Baptiste Roziere, Bethany Biron, Binh Tang, Bobbie Chern, Charlotte Caucheteux, Chaya Nayak, Chloe Bi, Chris Marra, Chris McConnell, Christian Keller, Christophe Touret, Chunyang Wu, Corinne Wong, Cristian Canton Ferrer, Cyrus Nikolaidis, Damien Allonsius, Daniel Song, Danielle Pintz, Danny Livshits, David Esiobu, Dhruv Choudhary, Dhruv Mahajan, Diego Garcia-Olano, Diego Perino, Dieuwke Hupkes, Egor Lakomkin, Ehab AlBadawy, Elina Lobanova, Emily Dinan, Eric Michael Smith, Filip Radenovic, Frank Zhang, Gabriel Synnaeve, Gabrielle Lee, Georgia Lewis Anderson, Graeme Nail, Gregoire Mialon, Guan Pang, Guillem Cucurell, Hailey Nguyen, Hannah Korevaar, Hu Xu, Hugo Touvron, Iliyan Zarov, Imanol Arrieta Ibarra, Isabel Kloumann, Ishan Misra, Ivan Evtimov, Jade Copet, Jaewon Lee, Jan Geffert, Jana Vranes, Jason Park, Jay Mahadeokar, Jeet Shah, Jelmer van der Linde, Jennifer Billock, Jenny Hong, Jenya Lee, Jeremy Fu, Jianfeng Chi, Jianyu Huang, Jiawen

Liu, Jie Wang, Jiecao Yu, Joanna Bitton, Joe Spisak, Jongsoo Park, Joseph Rocca, Joshua Johnstun, Joshua Saxe, Junteng Jia, Kalyan Vasuden Alwala, Kartikeya Upasani, Kate Plawiak, Ke Li, Kenneth Heafield, Kevin Stone, Khalid El-Arini, Krithika Iyer, Kshitiz Malik, Kuenley Chiu, Kunal Bhalla, Lauren Rantala-Yeary, Laurens van der Maaten, Lawrence Chen, Liang Tan, Liz Jenkins, Louis Martin, Lovish Madaan, Lubo Malo, Lukas Blecher, Lukas Landzaat, Luke de Oliveira, Madeline Muzzi, Mahesh Pasupuleti, Mannat Singh, Manohar Paluri, Marcin Kardas, Mathew Oldham, Mathieu Rita, Maya Pavlova, Melanie Kambadur, Mike Lewis, Min Si, Mitesh Kumar Singh, Mona Hassan, Naman Goyal, Narjes Torabi, Nikolay Bashlykov, Nikolay Bogoychev, Niladri Chatterji, Olivier Duchenne, Onur Çelebi, Patrick Alrassy, Pengchuan Zhang, Pengwei Li, Petar Vasic, Peter Weng, Prajjwal Bhargava, Pratik Dubal, Praveen Krishnan, Punit Singh Koura, Puxin Xu, Qing He, Qingxiao Dong, Ragavan Srinivasan, Raj Ganapathy, Ramon Calderer, Ricardo Silveira Cabral, Robert Stojnic, Roberta Raileanu, Rohit Girdhar, Rohit Patel, Romain Sauvestre, Ronnie Polidoro, Roshan Sumbaly, Ross Taylor, Ruan Silva, Rui Hou, Rui Wang, Saghar Hosseini, Sahana Chennabasappa, Sanjay Singh, Sean Bell, Seohyun Sonia Kim, Sergey Edunov, Shaoliang Nie, Sharan Narang, Sharath Raparthy, Sheng Shen, Shengye Wan, Shruti Bhosale, Shun Zhang, Simon Vandenhende, Soumya Batra, Spencer Whitman, Sten Sootla, Stephane Collot, Suchin Gururangan, Sydney Borodinsky, Tamar Herman, Tara Fowler, Tarek Sheasha, Thomas Georgiou, Thomas Scialom, Tobias Speckbacher, Todor Mihaylov, Tong Xiao, Ujjwal Karn, Vedanuj Goswami, Vibhor Gupta, Vignesh Ramanathan, Viktor Kerkez, Vincent Gonguet, Virginie Do, Vish Vogeti, Vladan Petrovic, Weiwei Chu, Wenhan Xiong, Wenyin Fu, Whitney Meers, Xavier Martinet, Xiaodong Wang, Xiaoqing Ellen Tan, Xinfeng Xie, Xuchao Jia, Xuewei Wang, Yaelle Goldschlag, Yashesh Gaur, Yasmine Babaei, Yi Wen, Yiwen Song, Yuchen Zhang, Yue Li, Yuning Mao, Zacharie Delpierre Coudert, Zheng Yan, Zhengxing Chen, Zoe Papakipos, Aaditya Singh, Aaron Grattafiori, Abha Jain, Adam Kelsey, Adam Shajnfeld, Adithya Gangidi, Adolfo Victoria, Ahuva Goldstand, Ajay Menon, Ajay Sharma, Alex Boesenberg, Alex Vaughan, Alexei Baevski, Allie Feinstein, Amanda Kallet, Amit Sangani, Anam Yunus, Andrei Lupu, Andres Alvarado, Andrew Caples, Andrew Gu, Andrew Ho, Andrew Poulton, Andrew Ryan, Ankit Ramchandani, Annie Franco, Aparajita Saraf, Arkabandhu Chowdhury, Ashley Gabriel, Ashwin Bharambe, Assaf Eisenman, Azadeh Yazdan, Beau James, Ben Maurer, Benjamin Leonhardi, Bernie Huang, Beth Loyd, Beto De Paola, Bhargavi Paranjape, Bing Liu, Bo Wu, Boyu Ni, Braden Hancock, Bram Wasti, Brandon Spence, Brani Stojkovic, Brian Gamido, Britt Montalvo, Carl Parker, Carly Burton, Catalina Mejia, Changhan Wang, Changkyu Kim, Chao Zhou, Chester Hu, Ching-Hsiang Chu, Chris Cai, Chris Tindal, Christoph Feichtenhofer, Damon Civin, Dana Beaty, Daniel Kreymer, Daniel Li, Danny Wyatt, David Adkins, David Xu, Davide Testuggine, Delia David, Devi Parikh, Diana Liskovich, Didem Foss, Dingkang Wang, Duc Le, Dustin Holland, Edward Dowling, Eissa Jamil, Elaine Montgomery, Eleonora Presani, Emily Hahn, Emily Wood, Erik Brinkman, Esteban Arcaute, Evan Dunbar, Evan Smothers, Fei Sun, Felix Kreuk, Feng Tian, Firat Ozgenel, Francesco Caggioni, Francisco Guzmán, Frank Kanayet, Frank Seide, Gabriela Medina Florez, Gabriella Schwarz, Gada Badeer, Georgia Swee, Gil Halpern, Govind Thattai, Grant Herman, Grigory Sizov, Guangyi, Zhang, Guna Lakshminarayanan, Hamid Shojanazeri, Han Zou, Hannah Wang, Hanwen Zha, Haroun Habeeb, Harrison Rudolph, Helen Suk, Henry Aspegren, Hunter Goldman, Ibrahim Damlaj, Igor Molybog, Igor Tufanov, Irina-Elena Veliche, Itai Gat, Jake Weissman, James Geboski, James Kohli, Japhet Asher, Jean-Baptiste Gaya, Jeff Marcus, Jeff Tang, Jennifer Chan, Jenny Zhen, Jeremy Reizenstein, Jeremy Teboul, Jessica Zhong, Jian Jin, Jingyi Yang, Joe Cummings, Jon Carvill, Jon Shepard, Jonathan McPhie, Jonathan Torres, Josh Ginsburg, Junjie Wang, Kai Wu, Kam Hou U, Karan Saxena, Karthik Prasad, Kartikay Khandelwal, Katayoun Zand, Kathy Matosich, Kaushik Veeraraghavan, Kelly Michelena, Keqian Li, Kun Huang, Kunal Chawla, Kushal Lakhotia, Kyle Huang, Lailin Chen, Lakshya Garg, Lavender A, Leandro Silva, Lee Bell, Lei Zhang, Liangpeng Guo, Licheng Yu, Liron Moshkovich, Luca Wehrstedt, Madian Khabsa, Manav Avalani, Manish Bhatt, Maria Tsimpoukelli, Martynas Mankus, Matan Hasson, Matthew Lennie, Matthias Reso, Maxim Groshev, Maxim Naumov, Maya Lathi, Meghan Keneally, Michael L. Seltzer, Michal Valko, Michelle Restrepo, Mihir Patel, Mik Vyatskov, Mikayel Samvelyan, Mike Clark, Mike Macey, Mike Wang, Miquel Jubert Hermoso, Mo Metanat, Mohammad Rastegari, Munish Bansal, Nandhini Santhanam, Natascha Parks, Natasha White, Navyata Bawa, Nayan Singhal, Nick Egebo, Nicolas Usunier, Nikolay Pavlovich Laptev, Ning Dong, Ning Zhang, Norman Cheng, Oleg Chernoguz, Olivia Hart, Omkar Salpekar, Ozlem Kalinli, Parkin Kent, Parth Parekh, Paul Saab, Pavan Balaji, Pedro Rittner, Philip Bontrager, Pierre Roux, Piotr Dollar, Polina Zvyagina, Prashant Ratanchandani, Pritish Yuvraj, Qian Liang, Rachad Alao, Rachel Rodriguez, Rafi Ayub, Raghotham Murthy, Raghu Nayani, Rahul Mitra, Raymond Li, Rebekkah Hogan, Robin Battey, Rocky Wang, Rohan Maheswari, Russ Howes, Ruty Rinott, Sai Jayesh Bondu, Samyak Datta, Sara Chugh, Sara Hunt, Sargun Dhillon, Sasha Sidorov, Satadru Pan, Saurabh Verma, Seiji Yamamoto, Sharadh Ramaswamy, Shaun Lindsay, Shaun Lindsay, Sheng Feng, Shenghao Lin, Shengxin Cindy Zha, Shiva Shankar, Shuqiang Zhang, Shuqiang Zhang, Sinong Wang, Sneha Agarwal, Soji Sajuyigbe, Soumith Chintala, Stephanie Max, Stephen Chen, Steve Kehoe, Steve Satterfield, Sudarshan Govindaprasad, Sumit Gupta, Sungmin Cho, Sunny Virk, Suraj Subramanian, Sy Choudhury, Sydney Goldman, Tal Remez, Tamar Glaser, Tamara Best, Thilo Kohler, Thomas Robinson, Tianhe Li, Tianjun Zhang, Tim Matthews, Timothy Chou, Tzook Shaked, Varun Vontimitta, Victoria Ajayi, Victoria Montanez, Vijai Mohan, Vinay Satish Kumar, Vishal Mangla, Vítor Albiero, Vlad Ionescu, Vlad Poenaru, Vlad Tiberiu Mihailescu, Vladimir Ivanov, Wei Li, Wenchen Wang, Wenwen Jiang, Wes Bouaziz, Will Constable, Xiaocheng Tang, Xiaofang Wang, Xiaojian Wu, Xiaolan Wang, Xide Xia, Xilun Wu, Xinbo Gao, Yanjun Chen, Ye Hu, Ye Jia, Ye Qi, Yenda Li, Yilin Zhang, Ying Zhang, Yossi Adi, Youngjin Nam, Yu, Wang, Yuchen Hao, Yundi Qian, Yuzi He, Zach Rait, Zachary DeVito, Zef Rosnbrick, Zhaoduo Wen, Zhenyu Yang, and Zhiwei Zhao. 2024. The llama 3 herd of models.

Christian Grévisse. 2024. Llm-based automatic short answer grading in undergraduate medical education. *BMC Medical Education*, 24(1):1060.

Veronika Hackl, Alexandra Elena Müller, Michael Granitzer, and Maximilian Sailer. 2023. Is gpt-4 a reliable rater? evaluating consistency in gpt-4's text ratings. In *Frontiers in Education*, volume 8, page 1272229. Frontiers Media SA.

Rositsa V Ivanova and Siegfried Handschuh. 2024. Evaluating llms' performance at automatic short-answer grading.

Albert Q. Jiang, Alexandre Sablayrolles, Arthur Mensch, Chris Bamford, Devendra Singh Chaplot, Diego de las Casas, Florian Bressand, Gianna Lengyel, Guillaume Lample, Lucile Saulnier, Lélio Renard Lavaud, Marie-Anne Lachaux, Pierre Stock, Teven Le Scao, Thibaut Lavril, Thomas Wang, Timothée Lacroix, and William El Sayed. 2023. Mistral 7b.

Artur Kiulian, Anton Polishko, Mykola Khandoga, Oryna Chubych, Jack Connor, Raghav Ravishankar, and Adarsh Shirawalmath. 2024. From bytes to borsch: Fine-tuning gemma and mistral for the ukrainian language representation. *arXiv preprint arXiv:2404.09138*.

Pernille Andresen Klevstuen. 2022. Assisting efficient and fair grading with information retrieval and text mining techniques. Master's thesis, NTNU.

R Krithika and Jayasree Narayanan. 2015. Learning to grade short answers using machine learning techniques. In *Proceedings of the Third International Symposium on Women in Computing and Informatics*, pages 262–271.

VD Lai, NT Ngo, APB Veyseh, H Man, F Dernoncourt, T Bui, and TH Nguyen. 2023. Chatgpt beyond english: Towards a comprehensive evaluation of large language models in multilingual learning. arxiv.

Kristīne Levāne-Petrova, Roberts Darģis, Kristīne Pokratniece, and Viesturs Jūlijs Lasmanis. 2023. Balanced corpus of modern latvian (LVK2022). CLARIN-LV digital library at IMCS, University of Latvia.

Pedro Henrique Martins, Patrick Fernandes, João Alves, Nuno M. Guerreiro, Ricardo Rei, Duarte M. Alves, José Pombal, Amin Farajian, Manuel Faysse, Mateusz Klimaszewski, Pierre Colombo, Barry Haddow, José G. C. de Souza, Alexandra Birch, and André F. T. Martins. 2024. Eurollm: Multilingual language models for europe.

Tim Metzler, Paul G. Plöger, and Jörn Hees. 2024. Computer-assisted short answer grading using large language models and rubrics. In *INFORMATIK 2024*, pages 1383–1393. Gesellschaft für Informatik e.V., Bonn.

Atsushi Mizumoto and Masaki Eguchi. 2023. Exploring the potential of using an ai language model for automated essay scoring. *Research Methods in Applied Linguistics*, 2(2):100050.

Lekshmi R Pillai, G Veena, and Deepa Gupta. 2018. A combined approach using semantic role labelling and word sense disambiguation for question generation and answer extraction. In *2018 Second International Conference on Advances in Electronics, Computers and Communications (ICAECC)*, pages 1–6. IEEE.

Johannes Schneider, Bernd Schenk, and Christina Niklaus. 2023. Towards llm-based autograding for short textual answers. *arXiv preprint arXiv:2309.11508*.

V Sreevidhya and Jayasree Narayanan. 2021. Short descriptive answer evaluation using word-embedding techniques. In *2021 12th international conference on computing communication and networking technologies (ICCCNT)*, pages 1–4. IEEE.

Pavel Stefanovič, Birutė Pliuskuvienė, Urtė Radvilaitė, and Simona Ramanauskaitė. 2024. Machine learning model for chatgpt usage detection in students' answers to open-ended questions: Case of lithuanian language. *Education and Information Technologies*, pages 1–23.

Chul Sung, Tejas Dhamecha, Swarnadeep Saha, Tengfei Ma, Vinay Reddy, and Rishi Arora. 2019. Pre-training bert on domain resources for short answer grading. In *Proceedings of the 2019 Conference on Empirical Methods in Natural Language Processing and the 9th International Joint Conference on Natural Language Processing (EMNLP-IJCNLP)*, pages 6071–6075.

Gemini Team, Petko Georgiev, Ving Ian Lei, Ryan Burnell, Libin Bai, Anmol Gulati, Garrett Tanzer, Damien Vincent, Zhufeng Pan, Shibo Wang, Soroosh Mariooryad, Yifan Ding, Xinyang Geng, Fred Alcober, Roy Frostig, Mark Omernick, Lexi Walker, Cosmin Paduraru, Christina Sorokin, Andrea Tacchetti, Colin Gaffney, Samira Daruki, Olcan Sercinoglu, Zach Gleicher, Juliette Love, Paul

Voigtlaender, Rohan Jain, Gabriela Surita, Kareem Mohamed, Rory Blevins, Junwhan Ahn, Tao Zhu, Kornraphop Kawintiranon, Orhan Firat, Yiming Gu, Yujing Zhang, Matthew Rahtz, Manaal Faruqui, Natalie Clay, Justin Gilmer, JD Co-Reyes, Ivo Penchev, Rui Zhu, Nobuyuki Morioka, Kevin Hui, Krishna Haridasan, Victor Campos, Mahdis Mahdieh, Mandy Guo, Samer Hassan, Kevin Kilgour, Arpi Vezer, Heng-Tze Cheng, Raoul de Liedekerke, Siddharth Goyal, Paul Barham, DJ Strouse, Seb Noury, Jonas Adler, Mukund Sundararajan, Sharad Vikram, Dmitry Lepikhin, Michela Paganini, Xavier Garcia, Fan Yang, Dasha Valter, Maja Trebacz, Kiran Vodrahalli, Chulayuth Asawaroengchai, Roman Ring, Norbert Kalb, Livio Baldini Soares, Siddhartha Brahma, David Steiner, Tianhe Yu, Fabian Mentzer, Antoine He, Lucas Gonzalez, Bibo Xu, Raphael Lopez Kaufman, Laurent El Shafey, Junhyuk Oh, Tom Hennigan, George van den Driessche, Seth Odoom, Mario Lucic, Becca Roelofs, Sid Lall, Amit Marathe, Betty Chan, Santiago Ontanon, Luheng He, Denis Teplyashin, Jonathan Lai, Phil Crone, Bogdan Damoc, Lewis Ho, Sebastian Riedel, Karel Lenc, Chih-Kuan Yeh, Aakanksha Chowdhery, Yang Xu, Mehran Kazemi, Ehsan Amid, Anastasia Petrushkina, Kevin Swersky, Ali Khodaei, Gowoon Chen, Chris Larkin, Mario Pinto, Geng Yan, Adria Puigdomenech Badia, Piyush Patil, Steven Hansen, Dave Orr, Sebastien M. R. Arnold, Jordan Grimstad, Andrew Dai, Sholto Douglas, Rishika Sinha, Vikas Yadav, Xi Chen, Elena Gribovskaya, Jacob Austin, Jeffrey Zhao, Kaushal Patel, Paul Komarek, Sophia Austin, Sebastian Borgeaud, Linda Friso, Abhimanyu Goyal, Ben Caine, Kris Cao, Da-Woon Chung, Matthew Lamm, Gabe Barth-Maron, Thais Kagohara, Kate Olszewska, Mia Chen, Kaushik Shivakumar, Rishabh Agarwal, Harshal Godhia, Ravi Rajwar, Javier Snaider, Xerxes Dotiwalla, Yuan Liu, Aditya Barua, Victor Ungureanu, Yuan Zhang, Bat-Orgil Batsaikhan, Mateo Wirth, James Qin, Ivo Danihelka, Tulsee Doshi, Martin Chadwick, Jilin Chen, Sanil Jain, Quoc Le, Arjun Kar, Madhu Gurumurthy, Cheng Li, Ruoxin Sang, Fangyu Liu, Lampros Lamprou, Rich Munoz, Nathan Lintz, Harsh Mehta, Heidi Howard, Malcolm Reynolds, Lora Aroyo, Quan Wang, Lorenzo Blanco, Albin Cassirer, Jordan Griffith, Dipanjan Das, Stephan Lee, Jakub Sygnowski, Zach Fisher, James Besley, Richard Powell, Zafarali Ahmed, Dominik Paulus, David Reitter, Zalan Borsos, Rishabh Joshi, Aedan Pope, Steven Hand, Vittorio Selo, Vihan Jain, Nikhil Sethi, Megha Goel, Takaki Makino, Rhys May, Zhen Yang, Johan Schalkwyk, Christina Butterfield, Anja Hauth, Alex Goldin, Will Hawkins, Evan Senter, Sergey Brin, Oliver Woodman, Marvin Ritter, Eric Noland, Minh Giang, Vijay Bolina, Lisa Lee, Tim Blyth, Ian Mackinnon, Machel Reid, Obaid Sarvana, David Silver, Alexander Chen, Lily Wang, Loren Maggiore, Oscar Chang, Nithya Attaluri, Gregory Thornton, Chung-Cheng Chiu, Oskar Bunyan, Nir Levine, Timothy Chung, Evgenii Eltyshev, Xiance Si, Timothy Lillicrap, Demetra Brady, Vaibhav Aggarwal, Boxi Wu, Yuanzhong Xu, Ross McIlroy, Kartikeya Badola, Paramjit Sandhu, Erica Moreira, Wojciech Stokowiec, Ross Hemsley, Dong Li, Alex Tudor, Pranav Shyam, Elahe Rahimtoroghi, Salem Haykal, Pablo Sprechmann, Xiang Zhou, Diana Mincu, Yujia Li, Ravi Addanki, Kalpesh Krishna, Xiao Wu, Alexandre Frechette, Matan Eyal, Allan Dafoe, Dave Lacey, Jay Whang, Thi Avrahami, Ye Zhang, Emanuel Taropa, Hanzhao Lin, Daniel Toyama, Eliza Rutherford, Motoki Sano, HyunJeong Choe, Alex Tomala, Chalence Safranek-Shrader, Nora Kassner, Mantas Pajarskas, Matt Harvey, Sean Sechrist, Meire Fortunato, Christina Lyu, Gamaleldin Elsayed, Chenkai Kuang, James Lottes, Eric Chu, Chao Jia, Chih-Wei Chen, Peter Humphreys, Kate Baumli, Connie Tao, Rajkumar Samuel, Cicero Nogueira dos Santos, Anders Andreassen, Nemanja Rakićević, Dominik Grewe, Aviral Kumar, Stephanie Winkler, Jonathan Caton, Andrew Brock, Sid Dalmia, Hannah Sheahan, Iain Barr, Yingjie Miao, Paul Natsev, Jacob Devlin, Feryal Behbahani, Flavien Prost, Yanhua Sun, Artiom Myaskovsky, Thanumalayan Sankaranarayana Pillai, Dan Hurt, Angeliki Lazaridou, Xi Xiong, Ce Zheng, Fabio Pardo, Xiaowei Li, Dan Horgan, Joe Stanton, Moran Ambar, Fei Xia, Alejandro Lince, Mingqiu Wang, Basil Mustafa, Albert Webson, Hyo Lee, Rohan Anil, Martin Wicke, Timothy Dozat, Abhishek Sinha, Enrique Piqueras, Elahe Dabir, Shyam Upadhyay, Anudhyan Boral, Lisa Anne Hendricks, Corey Fry, Josip Djolonga, Yi Su, Jake Walker, Jane Labanowski, Ronny Huang, Vedant Misra, Jeremy Chen, RJ Skerry-Ryan, Avi Singh, Shruti Rijhwani, Dian Yu, Alex Castro-Ros, Beer Changpinyo, Romina Datta, Sumit Bagri, Arnar Mar Hrafnkelsson, Marcello Maggioni, Daniel Zheng, Yury Sulsky, Shaobo Hou, Tom Le Paine, Antoine Yang, Jason Riesa, Dominika Rogozinska, Dror Marcus, Dalia El Badawy, Qiao Zhang, Luyu Wang, Helen Miller, Jeremy Greer, Lars Lowe Sjos, Azade Nova, Heiga Zen, Rahma Chaabouni, Mihaela Rosca, Jiepu Jiang, Charlie Chen, Ruibo Liu, Tara Sainath, Maxim Krikun, Alex Polozov, Jean-Baptiste Lespiau, Josh Newlan, Zeyncep Cankara, Soo Kwak, Yunhan Xu, Phil Chen, Andy Coenen, Clemens Meyer, Katerina Tsihlas, Ada Ma, Juraj Gottweis, Jinwei Xing, Chenjie Gu, Jin Miao, Christian Frank, Zeynep Cankara, Sanjay Ganapathy, Ishita Dasgupta, Steph Hughes-Fitt, Heng Chen, David Reid, Keran Rong, Hongmin Fan, Joost van Amersfoort, Vincent Zhuang, Aaron Cohen, Shixiang Shane Gu, Anhad Mohananey, Anastasija Ilic, Taylor Tobin, John Wieting, Anna Bortsova, Phoebe Thacker, Emma Wang, Emily Caveness, Justin Chiu, Eren Sezener, Alex Kaskasoli, Steven Baker, Katie Millican, Mohamed Elhawaty, Kostas Aisopos, Carl Lebsack, Nathan Byrd, Hanjun Dai, Wenhao Jia, Matthew Wiethoff, Elnaz Davoodi, Albert Weston, Lakshman Yagati, Arun Ahuja, Isabel Gao, Golan Pundak, Susan Zhang, Michael Azzam, Khe Chai Sim, Sergi Caelles, James Keeling, Abhanshu Sharma, Andy Swing, YaGuang Li, Chenxi Liu, Carrie Grimes

Bostock, Yamini Bansal, Zachary Nado, Ankesh Anand, Josh Lipschultz, Abhijit Karmarkar, Lev Proleev, Abe Ittycheriah, Soheil Hassas Yeganeh, George Polovets, Aleksandra Faust, Jiao Sun, Alban Rrustemi, Pen Li, Rakesh Shivanna, Jeremiah Liu, Chris Welty, Federico Lebron, Anirudh Baddepudi, Sebastian Krause, Emilio Parisotto, Radu Soricut, Zheng Xu, Dawn Bloxwich, Melvin Johnson, Behnam Neyshabur, Justin Mao-Jones, Renshen Wang, Vinay Ramasesh, Zaheer Abbas, Arthur Guez, Constant Segal, Duc Dung Nguyen, James Svensson, Le Hou, Sarah York, Kieran Milan, Sophie Bridgers, Wiktor Gworek, Marco Tagliasacchi, James Lee-Thorp, Michael Chang, Alexey Guseynov, Ale Jakse Hartman, Michael Kwong, Ruizhe Zhao, Sheleem Kashem, Elizabeth Cole, Antoine Miech, Richard Tanburn, Mary Phuong, Filip Pavetic, Sebastien Cevey, Ramona Comanescu, Richard Ives, Sherry Yang, Cosmo Du, Bo Li, Zizhao Zhang, Mariko Iinuma, Clara Huiyi Hu, Aurko Roy, Shaan Bijwadia, Zhenkai Zhu, Danilo Martins, Rachel Saputro, Anita Gergely, Steven Zheng, Dawei Jia, Ioannis Antonoglou, Adam Sadovsky, Shane Gu, Yingying Bi, Alek Andreev, Sina Samangooei, Mina Khan, Tomas Kocisky, Angelos Filos, Chintu Kumar, Colton Bishop, Adams Yu, Sarah Hodkinson, Sid Mittal, Premal Shah, Alexandre Moufarek, Yong Cheng, Adam Bloniarz, Jaehoon Lee, Pedram Pejman, Paul Michel, Stephen Spencer, Vladimir Feinberg, Xuehan Xiong, Nikolay Savinov, Charlotte Smith, Siamak Shakeri, Dustin Tran, Mary Chesus, Bernd Bohnet, George Tucker, Tamara von Glehn, Carrie Muir, Yiran Mao, Hideto Kazawa, Ambrose Slone, Kedar Soparkar, Disha Shrivastava, James Cobon-Kerr, Michael Sharman, Jay Pavagadhi, Carlos Araya, Karolis Misiunas, Nimesh Ghelani, Michael Laskin, David Barker, Qiujia Li, Anton Briukhov, Neil Houlsby, Mia Glaese, Balaji Lakshminarayanan, Nathan Schucher, Yunhao Tang, Eli Collins, Hyeontaek Lim, Fangxiaoyu Feng, Adria Recasens, Guangda Lai, Alberto Magni, Nicola De Cao, Aditya Siddhant, Zoe Ashwood, Jordi Orbay, Mostafa Dehghani, Jenny Brennan, Yifan He, Kelvin Xu, Yang Gao, Carl Saroufim, James Molloy, Xinyi Wu, Seb Arnold, Solomon Chang, Julian Schrittwieser, Elena Buchatskaya, Soroush Radpour, Martin Polacek, Skye Giordano, Ankur Bapna, Simon Tokumine, Vincent Hellendoorn, Thibault Sottiaux, Sarah Cogan, Aliaksei Severyn, Mohammad Saleh, Shantanu Thakoor, Laurent Shefey, Siyuan Qiao, Meenu Gaba, Shuo yiin Chang, Craig Swanson, Biao Zhang, Benjamin Lee, Paul Kishan Rubenstein, Gan Song, Tom Kwiatkowski, Anna Koop, Ajay Kannan, David Kao, Parker Schuh, Axel Stjerngren, Golnaz Ghiasi, Gena Gibson, Luke Vilnis, Ye Yuan, Felipe Tiengo Ferreira, Aishwarya Kamath, Ted Klimenko, Ken Franko, Kefan Xiao, Indro Bhattacharya, Miteyan Patel, Rui Wang, Alex Morris, Robin Strudel, Vivek Sharma, Peter Choy, Sayed Hadi Hashemi, Jessica Landon, Mara Finkelstein, Priya Jhakra, Justin Frye, Megan Barnes, Matthew Mauger, Dennis Daun, Khuslen Baatarsukh, Matthew Tung, Wael Farhan, Henryk Michalewski, Fabio Viola, Felix de Chaumont Quitry, Charline Le Lan, Tom Hudson, Qingze Wang, Felix Fischer, Ivy Zheng, Elspeth White, Anca Dragan, Jean baptiste Alayrac, Eric Ni, Alexander Pritzel, Adam Iwanicki, Michael Isard, Anna Bulanova, Lukas Zilka, Ethan Dyer, Devendra Sachan, Srivatsan Srinivasan, Hannah Muckenhirn, Honglong Cai, Amol Mandhane, Mukarram Tariq, Jack W. Rae, Gary Wang, Kareem Ayoub, Nicholas FitzGerald, Yao Zhao, Woohyun Han, Chris Alberti, Dan Garrette, Kashyap Krishnakumar, Mai Gimenez, Anselm Levskaya, Daniel Sohn, Josip Matak, Inaki Iturrate, Michael B. Chang, Jackie Xiang, Yuan Cao, Nishant Ranka, Geoff Brown, Adrian Hutter, Vahab Mirrokni, Nanxin Chen, Kaisheng Yao, Zoltan Egyed, Francois Galilee, Tyler Liechty, Praveen Kallakuri, Evan Palmer, Sanjay Ghemawat, Jasmine Liu, David Tao, Chloe Thornton, Tim Green, Mimi Jasarevic, Sharon Lin, Victor Cotruta, Yi-Xuan Tan, Noah Fiedel, Hongkun Yu, Ed Chi, Alexander Neitz, Jens Heitkaemper, Anu Sinha, Denny Zhou, Yi Sun, Charbel Kaed, Brice Hulse, Swaroop Mishra, Maria Georgaki, Sneha Kudugunta, Clement Farabet, Izhak Shafran, Daniel Vlasic, Anton Tsitsulin, Rajagopal Ananthanarayanan, Alen Carin, Guolong Su, Pei Sun, Shashank V, Gabriel Carvajal, Josef Broder, Iulia Comsa, Alena Repina, William Wong, Warren Weilun Chen, Peter Hawkins, Egor Filonov, Lucia Loher, Christoph Hirnschall, Weiyi Wang, Jingchen Ye, Andrea Burns, Hardie Cate, Diana Gage Wright, Federico Piccinini, Lei Zhang, Chu-Cheng Lin, Ionel Gog, Yana Kulizhskaya, Ashwin Sreevatsa, Shuang Song, Luis C. Cobo, Anand Iyer, Chetan Tekur, Guillermo Garrido, Zhuyun Xiao, Rupert Kemp, Huaixiu Steven Zheng, Hui Li, Ananth Agarwal, Christel Ngani, Kati Goshvadi, Rebeca Santamaria-Fernandez, Wojciech Fica, Xinyun Chen, Chris Gorgolewski, Sean Sun, Roopal Garg, Xinyu Ye, S. M. Ali Eslami, Nan Hua, Jon Simon, Pratik Joshi, Yelin Kim, Ian Tenney, Sahitya Potluri, Lam Nguyen Thiet, Quan Yuan, Florian Luisier, Alexandra Chronopoulou, Salvatore Scellato, Praveen Srinivasan, Minmin Chen, Vinod Koverkathu, Valentin Dalibard, Yaming Xu, Brennan Saeta, Keith Anderson, Thibault Sellam, Nick Fernando, Fantine Huot, Junehyuk Jung, Mani Varadarajan, Michael Quinn, Amit Raul, Maigo Le, Ruslan Habalov, Jon Clark, Komal Jalan, Kalesha Bullard, Achintya Singhal, Thang Luong, Boyu Wang, Sujeevan Rajayogam, Julian Eisenschlos, Johnson Jia, Daniel Finchelstein, Alex Yakubovich, Daniel Balle, Michael Fink, Sameer Agarwal, Jing Li, Dj Dvijotham, Shalini Pal, Kai Kang, Jaclyn Konzelmann, Jennifer Beattie, Olivier Dousse, Diane Wu, Remi Crocker, Chen Elkind, Siddhartha Reddy Jonnalagadda, Jong Lee, Dan Holtmann-Rice, Krystal Kallarackal, Rosanne Liu, Denis Vnukov, Neera Vats, Luca Invernizzi, Mohsen Jafari, Huanjie Zhou, Lilly Taylor, Jennifer Prendki, Marcus Wu, Tom Eccles, Tianqi Liu, Kavya Kopparapu, Francoise Beaufays, Christof Angermueller, Andreea Marzoca, Shourya Sarcar,

Hilal Dib, Jeff Stanway, Frank Perbet, Nejc Trdin, Rachel Sterneck, Andrey Khorlin, Dinghua Li, Xihui Wu, Sonam Goenka, David Madras, Sasha Goldshtein, Willi Gierke, Tong Zhou, Yaxin Liu, Yannie Liang, Anais White, Yunjie Li, Shreya Singh, Sanaz Bahargam, Mark Epstein, Sujoy Basu, Li Lao, Adnan Ozturel, Carl Crous, Alex Zhai, Han Lu, Zora Tung, Neeraj Gaur, Alanna Walton, Lucas Dixon, Ming Zhang, Amir Globerson, Grant Uy, Andrew Bolt, Olivia Wiles, Milad Nasr, Ilia Shumailov, Marco Selvi, Francesco Piccinno, Ricardo Aguilar, Sara McCarthy, Misha Khalman, Mrinal Shukla, Vlado Galic, John Carpenter, Kevin Villela, Haibin Zhang, Harry Richardson, James Martens, Matko Bosnjak, Shreyas Rammohan Belle, Jeff Seibert, Mahmoud Alnahlawi, Brian McWilliams, Sankalp Singh, Annie Louis, Wen Ding, Dan Popovici, Lenin Simicich, Laura Knight, Pulkit Mehta, Nishesh Gupta, Chongyang Shi, Saaber Fatehi, Jovana Mitrovic, Alex Grills, Joseph Pagadora, Dessie Petrova, Danielle Eisenbud, Zhishuai Zhang, Damion Yates, Bhavishya Mittal, Nilesh Tripuraneni, Yannis Assael, Thomas Brovelli, Prateek Jain, Mihajlo Velimirovic, Canfer Akbulut, Jiaqi Mu, Wolfgang Macherey, Ravin Kumar, Jun Xu, Haroon Qureshi, Gheorghe Comanici, Jeremy Wiesner, Zhitao Gong, Anton Ruddock, Matthias Bauer, Nick Felt, Anirudh GP, Anurag Arnab, Dustin Zelle, Jonas Rothfuss, Bill Rosgen, Ashish Shenoy, Bryan Seybold, Xinjian Li, Jayaram Mudigonda, Goker Erdogan, Jiawei Xia, Jiri Simsa, Andrea Michi, Yi Yao, Christopher Yew, Steven Kan, Isaac Caswell, Carey Radebaugh, Andre Elisseeff, Pedro Valenzuela, Kay McKinney, Kim Paterson, Albert Cui, Eri Latorre-Chimoto, Solomon Kim, William Zeng, Ken Durden, Priya Ponnapalli, Tiberiu Sosea, Christopher A. Choquette-Choo, James Manyika, Brona Robenek, Harsha Vashisht, Sebastien Pereira, Hoi Lam, Marko Velic, Denese Owusu-Afriyie, Katherine Lee, Tolga Bolukbasi, Alicia Parrish, Shawn Lu, Jane Park, Balaji Venkatraman, Alice Talbert, Lambert Rosique, Yuchung Cheng, Andrei Sozanschi, Adam Paszke, Praveen Kumar, Jessica Austin, Lu Li, Khalid Salama, Wooyeol Kim, Nandita Dukkipati, Anthony Baryshnikov, Christos Kaplanis, XiangHai Sheng, Yuri Chervonyi, Caglar Unlu, Diego de Las Casas, Harry Askham, Kathryn Tunyasuvunakool, Felix Gimeno, Siim Poder, Chester Kwak, Matt Miecnikowski, Vahab Mirrokni, Alek Dimitriev, Aaron Parisi, Dangyi Liu, Tomy Tsai, Toby Shevlane, Christina Kouridi, Drew Garmon, Adrian Goedeckemeyer, Adam R. Brown, Anitha Vijayakumar, Ali Elqursh, Sadegh Jazayeri, Jin Huang, Sara Mc Carthy, Jay Hoover, Lucy Kim, Sandeep Kumar, Wei Chen, Courtney Biles, Garrett Bingham, Evan Rosen, Lisa Wang, Qijun Tan, David Engel, Francesco Pongetti, Dario de Cesare, Dongseong Hwang, Lily Yu, Jennifer Pullman, Srini Narayanan, Kyle Levin, Siddharth Gopal, Megan Li, Asaf Aharoni, Trieu Trinh, Jessica Lo, Norman Casagrande, Roopali Vij, Loic Matthey, Bramandia Ramadhana, Austin Matthews, CJ Carey, Matthew Johnson, Kremena Goranova, Rohin Shah, Shereen Ashraf, Kingshuk Dasgupta, Rasmus Larsen, Yicheng Wang, Manish Reddy Vuyyuru, Chong Jiang, Joana Ijazi, Kazuki Osawa, Celine Smith, Ramya Sree Boppana, Taylan Bilal, Yuma Koizumi, Ying Xu, Yasemin Altun, Nir Shabat, Ben Bariach, Alex Korchemniy, Kiam Choo, Olaf Ronneberger, Chimezie Iwuanyanwu, Shubin Zhao, David Soergel, Cho-Jui Hsieh, Irene Cai, Shariq Iqbal, Martin Sundermeyer, Zhe Chen, Elie Bursztein, Chaitanya Malaviya, Fadi Biadsy, Prakash Shroff, Inderjit Dhillon, Tejasi Latkar, Chris Dyer, Hannah Forbes, Massimo Nicosia, Vitaly Nikolaev, Somer Greene, Marin Georgiev, Pidong Wang, Nina Martin, Hanie Sedghi, John Zhang, Praseem Banzal, Doug Fritz, Vikram Rao, Xuezhi Wang, Jiageng Zhang, Viorica Patraucean, Dayou Du, Igor Mordatch, Ivan Jurin, Lewis Liu, Ayush Dubey, Abhi Mohan, Janek Nowakowski, Vlad-Doru Ion, Nan Wei, Reiko Tojo, Maria Abi Raad, Drew A. Hudson, Vaishakh Keshava, Shubham Agrawal, Kevin Ramirez, Zhichun Wu, Hoang Nguyen, Ji Liu, Madhavi Sewak, Bryce Petrini, DongHyun Choi, Ivan Philips, Ziyue Wang, Ioana Bica, Ankush Garg, Jarek Wilkiewicz, Priyanka Agrawal, Xiaowei Li, Danhao Guo, Emily Xue, Naseer Shaik, Andrew Leach, Sadh MNM Khan, Julia Wiesinger, Sammy Jerome, Abhishek Chakladar, Alek Wenjiao Wang, Tina Ornduff, Folake Abu, Alireza Ghaffarkhah, Marcus Wainwright, Mario Cortes, Frederick Liu, Joshua Maynez, Andreas Terzis, Pouya Samangouei, Riham Mansour, Tomasz Kepa, François-Xavier Aubet, Anton Algymr, Dan Banica, Agoston Weisz, Andras Orban, Alexandre Senges, Ewa Andrejczuk, Mark Geller, Niccolo Dal Santo, Valentin Anklin, Majd Al Merey, Martin Baeuml, Trevor Strohman, Junwen Bai, Slav Petrov, Yonghui Wu, Demis Hassabis, Koray Kavukcuoglu, Jeffrey Dean, and Oriol Vinyals. 2024. Gemini 1.5: Unlocking multimodal understanding across millions of tokens of context.

Qwen Team. 2024. Qwen2.5: A party of foundation models.

Maximilian Tornqvist, Mosleh Mahamud, Erick Mendez Guzman, and Alexandra Farazouli. 2023. Exasag: Explainable framework for automatic short answer grading. In *Proceedings of the 18th Workshop on Innovative Use of NLP for Building Educational Applications (BEA 2023)*, pages 361–371.

Rebecka Weegar and Peter Idestam-Almquist. 2024. Reducing workload in short answer grading using machine learning. *International Journal of Artificial Intelligence in Education*, 34(2):247–273.

Nico Willms and Ulrike Padó. 2022. A transformer for sag: What does it grade? In *Swedish Language Technology Conference and NLP4CALL*, pages 114–122.

Kevin P Yancey, Geoffrey Laflair, Anthony Verardi, and Jill Burstein. 2023. Rating short l2 essays on the cefr scale with gpt-4. In *Proceedings of the 18th*

Workshop on Innovative Use of NLP for Building Educational Applications (BEA 2023), pages 576–584.

An Yang, Baosong Yang, Binyuan Hui, Bo Zheng, Bowen Yu, Chang Zhou, Chengpeng Li, Chengyuan Li, Dayiheng Liu, Fei Huang, Guanting Dong, Haoran Wei, Huan Lin, Jialong Tang, Jialin Wang, Jian Yang, Jianhong Tu, Jianwei Zhang, Jianxin Ma, Jin Xu, Jingren Zhou, Jinze Bai, Jinzheng He, Junyang Lin, Kai Dang, Keming Lu, Keqin Chen, Kexin Yang, Mei Li, Mingfeng Xue, Na Ni, Pei Zhang, Peng Wang, Ru Peng, Rui Men, Ruize Gao, Runji Lin, Shijie Wang, Shuai Bai, Sinan Tan, Tianhang Zhu, Tianhao Li, Tianyu Liu, Wenbin Ge, Xiaodong Deng, Xiaohuan Zhou, Xingzhang Ren, Xinyu Zhang, Xipin Wei, Xuancheng Ren, Yang Fan, Yang Yao, Yichang Zhang, Yu Wan, Yunfei Chu, Yuqiong Liu, Zeyu Cui, Zhenru Zhang, and Zhihao Fan. 2024. Qwen2 technical report. *arXiv preprint arXiv:2407.10671*.

Su-Youn Yoon. 2023. Short answer grading using one-shot prompting and text similarity scoring model. *arXiv preprint arXiv:2305.18638*.

M Zhang, S Baral, N Heffernan, and A Lan. Automatic short math answer grading via in-context meta-learning. arxiv 2022. *arXiv preprint arXiv:2205.15219*.

A Manual Evaluation

For each language, we recruited two native speakers to evaluate the outputs of LLMs on the answers generation task. Each annotator was presented with 360 random samples from the dataset. Each sample contained a question, a reference answer, a generated answer with an instruction on whether it supposed to be matched with the reference answer. If the reference answer and the generated answer are matched and they are supposed to be matched or the reference answer and the generated answer are not matched and they are not supposed to be matched, the label *accept* was assigned to the sample. Otherwise, the label *reject* was assigned. For each model (LLaMa2:13b, GPT-4o, and LLaMa3:7b) and for each matched generation type, the annotators were presented with 25 samples. For non-matched generation methods, the annotators were presented with 40 samples. The aggregated results (after cleaning the duplicates) are presented in the Table 3.

To calculate the inter-annotator agreement, we used Cohen Kappa score (Cohen, 1960) and an intersection ratio. One of the annotators per language was presented with additional 40 samples from the labeled dataset of the other annotator, including the equal coverage of models and generation methods in the data. The Cohen Kappa coefficient for Latvian language was 0.285 and the intersection score was of 0.825. The Cohen Kappa coefficient for Lithuanian language was 0.354 and the intersection score was of 0.82.

Based on the the results, we kept LLaMa3 Non-Match Relat. generation results and all of the GPT-4o generated results in the dataset for Lithuanian. Similarly, we kept LLaMa3 Non-Match Minor-Changes and GPT-4o (except for Match MoreInfo, which was excluded by mistake) in the dataset for Latvian. Our results indicate that GPT-4o is capable of generating matched and non-matched answers with different methods in these languages, when LLaMa3 and LLaMa2 struggle.

Lit R	Lit A	Lat R	Lat A	Model	Class
1	29	1	29	GPT-4o	Match Ents
0	30	4	26	GPT-4o	Match MoreInfo
1	29	2	28	GPT-4o	Match Syns
0	30	2	28	GPT-4o	Match Style
0	60	3	56	GPT-4o	Non-Match MinorCh.
3	57	2	57	GPT-4o	Non-Match Relat.
20	10	12	18	LLaMa2:13b	Match Ents
22	8	15	14	LLaMa2:13b	Match MoreInfo
13	17	10	19	LLaMa2:13b	Match Syns
12	18	14	16	LLaMa2:13b	Match Style
16	43	14	15	LLaMa2:13b	Non-Match MinorCh.
12	46	13	32	LLaMa2:13b	Non-Match Relat.
10	20	5	25	LLaMa3:7b	Match Ents
5	25	8	22	LLaMa3:7b	Match MoreInfo
8	22	3	26	LLaMa3:7b	Match Syns
13	16	14	16	LLaMa3:7b	Match Style
6	54	4	56	LLaMa3:7b	Non-Match MinorCh.
2	58	6	48	LLaMa3:7b	Non-Match Relat.
5	235	14	224	GPT-4o	All
95	142	79	144	LLaMa2:13b	All
44	195	40	193	LLaMa3:7b	All

Table 3: Annotation results. **R** and **A** indicate amount of rejected and accepted samples respectively with the language at the beginning. **Class** indicates a generation prompt that was used and whether it should match with the reference answer.

B Failure Cases Showcase

In this section, we present a sample of the samples per model and per generation rule, where the annotators marked the sample as incorrect, along with the annotator's comment on the decision if provided. The examples are provided in the subsections below.

B.1 Failure Examples for Lithuanian

Language / Rule: Lithuanian / M: Ents
Model Name: GPT-4o
Q (LT): Kokie buvo svarbiausi Kęstučio politiniai vaidmenys Lietuvos Didžiojoje Kunigaikštystėje ?
Q (EN): What were Kęstutis' most important political roles in the Grand Duchy of Lithuania?
Correct Answer (LT):Kęstutis užėmė keletą svarbių politinių vaidmenų. Jis buvo LDK submonarchas nuo 1337 ar 1345 m. iki 1381 m., o vėliau Lietuvos didysis kunigaikštis 1381–1382 m. Be to, jis valdė Gardiną ir Palenkę iki 1337 m., Žemaitiją nuo 1337 m., ir Trakus nuo 1337 ar 1345 m.
Correct Answer (EN): Kęstutis held several important political roles. He was a submonarch of the Grand Duchy of Lithuania from 1337 or 1345 to 1381, and later Grand Duke of Lithuania from 1381–1382. In addition, he ruled Grodno and Podlaskie until 1337, Samogitia from 1337, and Trakai from 1337 or 1345.
Generated (LT): Kęstutis turėjo keletą svarbių politinių pareigų Lietuvos Didžiojoje Kunigaikštystėje. Jis veikė kaip LDK submonarchas nuo 1337 arba 1345 iki 1381 metų prekybos su pagrindiniu Etijopija centru, o po to tapo Lietuvos didžiuoju kunigaikščiu nuo 1381 iki 1382 metų. Kitas svarbus postas buvo Gardino ir Palenkės valdymas iki 1337 metų, taip pat Žemaitijos valdymas nuo 1337 metų ir Trakų nuo 1337 arba 1345 metų.
Generated (EN): Kęstutis held several important political roles. He was a sub-monarch of the Grand Duchy of Lithuania from 1337 or 1345 to 1381, and later Grand Duke of Lithuania from 1381–1382. In addition, he ruled Grodno and Podlaskie until 1337, Samogitia from 1337, and Trakai from 1337 or 1345.
Comment: NA

Language / Rule: Lithuanian / M: Ents
Model Name: LLaMa3
Q (LT): Kodėl Valstiečių ir Naujosios demokratijos partijos susijungė 2001 metais?
Q (EN): On what occasions is it mandatory to sing or play the Lithuanian anthem?
Correct Answer (LT): Valstiečių ir Naujosios demokratijos partijos susijungė 2001 metais, siekdamos pagerinti savo pozicijas būsimuose rinkimuose ir tapti parlamentine partija. Valstiečių partijai grėsė likti regionine partija, turinčia įtakos tik rajonų savivaldybėse. Susijungimas pasiteisino - 2004 metais jungtinė partija gavo mandatą Europos Parlamente ir 10 mandatų Seime.
Correct Answer (EN): The Lithuanian anthem must be sung or played on various occasions, such as at the beginning and end of the Seimas sessions, at ceremonial meetings dedicated to Lithuanian holidays, when meeting foreign heads of state, when representing Lithuania abroad, on national television and radio broadcasts, and when raising the Lithuanian flag.
Generated (LT): Valstiečių ir Naujosios demokratijos partijos susijungimą 2001 metais galima aiškinti, jog tai buvo siekimas pagerinti pozicijas būsimuose rinkimuose ir tapti parlamentine partija. Valstiečių partija, kuri turėjo įtakos tik rajonų savivaldybėse, norėjo likti regionine partija, o susijungimas leido jiems dalyvauti Europos Parlamente ir Seime.
Generated (EN): The Lithuanian anthem must be sung or played when Lithuania celebrates its holidays, when the Seimas convenes, when meeting foreign heads of state, when representing the country abroad, on national television and radio broadcasts.
Comment: both wrong - grammar and logic

Language / Rule: Lithuanian / M: Ents
Model Name: LLaMa3
Q (LT): Kuo daugiausia minta baltieji gandrai?
Q (EN): What do white storks mainly eat?
Correct Answer (LT): Baltieji gandrai yra oportunistiniai "grobuonys", mintantys gausiausiais, beveik vien gyvūninės kilmės

maisto objektais. Jie gaudo vabzdžius, kitus bestuburius, žuvis, varliagyvius, ant žemės perinčių paukščių jauniklius. Kartais ryja peles, žiurkes, įvairius roplius, taip pat ir gyvates, neretai kiškių jauniklius ar net žebenkštis.
Correct Answer (EN): White storks are opportunistic "predators", feeding on the most abundant, almost exclusively animal-based food objects. They catch insects, other invertebrates, fish, amphibians, and ground-nesting bird chicks. Sometimes they devour mice, rats, various reptiles, as well as snakes, often hare chicks or even weasels.
Generated (LT): Baltieji gandrai yra panaudotinės "grobuonys", mintantys gausiausiais, beveik vien gyvūninės kilmės maisto objektais, tad jų šokas yra labai išvystytas. Jie gaudo vabzdžius, kitus bestuburius, žuvis, varliagyvius, ant žemės perinčių paukščių jauniklius.
Generated (EN): White storks are utilitarian "predators", feeding on the most abundant, almost exclusively animal-based food objects, so their shock is highly developed. They catch insects, other invertebrates, fish, amphibians, and ground-nesting bird chicks.
Comment: NA

Language / Rule: Lithuanian / M: Ents
Model Name: LlaMa2:13b
Q (LT): Kokias pareigas Algirdas Brazauskas ėjo nepriklausomoje Lietuvoje?
Q (EN): What positions did Algirdas Brazauskas hold in independent Lithuania?
Correct Answer (LT): Algirdas Brazauskas nepriklausomoje Lietuvoje ėjo prezidento (1992–1993 laikinai, 1993–1998 išrinktas) ir ministro pirmininko (2001–2006) pareigas.
Correct Answer (EN): Algirdas Brazauskas held the positions of President (1992–1993 interim, 1993–1998 elected) and Prime Minister (2001–2006) in independent Lithuania.
Generated (LT): Algirdas Brazauskas nepriklausomoje Lietuvoje ėjo prezidento ir ministro pirmininko pareigas, tokių kaip prezidentas (1992–1993 laikinai) ir ministra (2001–2006) pareigas.
Generated (EN): Algirdas Brazauskas held the positions of President and Prime Minister in independent Lithuania, such as President (1992–1993 interim) and Minister (2001–2006).
Comment: NA

Language / Rule: Lithuanian / M: Ents
Model Name: LLaMa2:13b
Q (LT): Kokios dvi seniūnaitijos priklauso Kernavės seniūnijai?
Q (EN): What two elderships belong to Kernavės eldership?
Correct Answer (LT): Kernavės seniūnijoje yra dvi seniūnaitijos: Kerniaus ir Piliakalnio.
Correct Answer (EN): There are two elderships in Kernavės eldership: Kerniaus and Piliakalnis.
Generated (LT): Kernavės seniūnijoje yra dvi seniūnaitijos: Kerniaus ir Piliakallio, tačiau tokių kaip Kernavės miestelė ir Piliakalnio savivaldybė.[Inst]
Generated (EN): There are two elderships in Kernavės eldership: Kerniaus and Piliakalnis, but such as Kernavės town and Piliakalnis municipality.
Comment: NA

Language / Rule: Lithuanian / M: Exclamatory
Model Name: LLaMa3
Q (LT): Kokias pareigas Algirdas Brazauskas ėjo nepriklausomoje Lietuvoje?
Q (EN): What positions did Algirdas Brazauskas hold in independent Lithuania?
Correct Answer (LT): Algirdas Brazauskas nepriklausomoje Lietuvoje ėjo prezidento (1992–1993 laikinai, 1993–1998 išrinktas) ir ministro pirmininko (2001–2006) pareigas.
Correct Answer (EN): In independent Lithuania, Algirdas Brazauskas held the positions of President (1992–1993 interim, 1993–1998 elected) and Prime Minister (2001–2006).
Generated (LT): Algirdas Brazauskas - tuo metu Lietuvos prezidentas ir ministras pirmininkas, atlikęs svarbias vietas nepriklausomoje šalyje!
Generated (EN): Algirdas Brazauskas - at that time the President and Prime Minister of Lithuania, who held important positions in the independent country!
Comment: NA

Language / Rule: Lithuanian / M: Exclamatory
Model Name: LLaMa3
Q (LT): Kada ir kodėl baigėsi pirmasis Kauno "Žalgirio" dominavimo laikotarpis LKL?
Q (EN): When and why did Kaunas Žalgiris' first period of dominance in the LKL end?
Correct Answer (LT): Kauno "Žalgirio" dominavimas, trukęs pirmuosius šešis sezonus (1993–1999 m.), baigėsi po jų pergalių Europos Taurės ir Eurolygos varžybose. Kitą sezoną (1999–2000 m.) LKL čempionais tapo Vilniaus "Lietuvos rytas".
Correct Answer (EN): Kaunas Žalgiris' dominance, which lasted for the first six seasons (1993–1999), ended after their victories in the European Cup and Euroleague. The next season (1999–2000), Vilnius Lietuvos rytas became the LKL champions.
Generated (LT): Kauno "Žalgirio" dominavimas baigėsi po šešių sezučių, kai jie pergudrio Europos Taurę ir Eurolygą, o po to Vilniaus "Lietuvos ryto" tapo LKL čempionais!
Generated (EN): Kaunas Žalgiris' dominance ended after six seasons, when they won the European Cup and Euroleague, and then Vilnius Lietuvos rytas became the LKL champions!
Comment: NA

Language / Rule: Lithuanian / M: Exclamatory
Model Name: LLaMa2:13b
Q (LT): Kokia yra Gedimino pilies atsiradimo legenda?
Q (EN): What is the legend of the origin of Gediminas Castle?
Correct Answer (LT): Legenda pasakoja, kad kunigaikštis Gediminas medžiodamas užmigo Šventaragio slėnyje ir susapnavo geležinį vilką, staugiantį ant kalno prie Neries ir Vilnios santakos. Žynys Lizdeika šį sapną išaiškino kaip pranašystę apie didžio miesto atsiradimą toje vietoje.
Correct Answer (EN): The legend says that Duke Gediminas fell asleep while hunting in the Šventaragis Valley and dreamed of an iron wolf howling on a mountain at the confluence of the Neris and Vilnius rivers. The seer Lizdeika interpreted this dream as a prophecy about the emergence of a great city in that place.
Generated (LT): Gediminas pilies atsiradimo legenda – pasaulinē istorija, kuriuo kalbējo apie kunigaikščį, ką ir kiek kito, susapnavo geležinį vilką ir šventaragio slēnyje
Generated (EN): The legend of the origin of Gediminas Castle is a world story that spoke about the duke, what and how much else, dreamed of an iron wolf and in the Šventaragis Valley
Comment: NA

Language / Rule: Lithuanian / M: Exclamatory
Model Name: LLaMa2:13b
Q (LT): Kada ir kokiomis aplinkybėmis Klaipėda buvo prijungta prie Lietuvos?
Q (EN): When and under what circumstances was Klaipėda annexed to Lithuania?
Correct Answer (LT): Klaipėda buvo prijungta prie Lietuvos 1923 m. po inscenizuoto sukilimo. Prieš tai miestas buvo atskirtas nuo Vokietijos pagal Versalio taikos sutartį po Pirmojo pasaulinio karo.
Correct Answer (EN): Klaipėda was annexed to Lithuania in 1923 after a staged uprising. Before that, the city was separated from Germany under the Treaty of Versailles after World War I.
Generated (LT): Klaipėda buvo prieš 1923 m. prijungta prie Lietuvos, po inscenizuoto sukilimo, prisijungant Vokietijo pagal Versalio taikos sutartį po Pirmojo pasaulinio karo
Generated (EN): Klaipėda was annexed to Lithuania before 1923, after a staged uprising, with the accession of Germany under the Treaty of Versailles after World War I.
Comment: NA

Language / Rule: Lithuanian / M: Synonyms
Model Name: GPT-4o
Q (LT): Kada ir kokiomis aplinkybėmis Klaipėdos kraštas buvo atskirtas nuo Vokietijos?
Q (EN): When and under what circumstances was the Klaipėda region separated from Germany?
Correct Answer (LT): Klaipėdos kraštas buvo atskirtas nuo Vokietijos 1919 metais pa-

gal Versalio taikos sutartį. Ši sutartis numatė, kad šiaurinė Rytų Prūsijos dalis, kuri ir tapo Klaipėdos kraštu, būtų atskirta nuo Vokietijos ir perduota sąjungininkų valstybių žinion. Šis sprendimas buvo priimtas po Paryžiaus taikos konferencijos, kurioje Lenkijos atstovas iš pradžių reikalavo Mažąją Lietuvą sujungti su Didžiąja ir abi prijungti prie Lenkijos, bet vėliau pasiūlė prie Lietuvos prijungti tik Klaipėdos kraštą, kuris iki Lietuvos ir Lenkijos sąjungos turėtų būti Antantės kontrolėje.
Correct Answer (EN): The Klaipėda region was separated from Germany in 1919 under the Treaty of Versailles. This treaty provided that the northern part of East Prussia, which became the Klaipėda region, would be separated from Germany and transferred to the control of the Allied powers. This decision was made after the Paris Peace Conference, where the Polish representative initially demanded that Lithuania Minor be united with Lithuania Major and both be annexed to Poland, but later proposed that only the Klaipėda region be annexed to Lithuania, which should have been under the control of the Entente until the union of Lithuania and Poland.
Generated (LT): 1919 metais, remiantis Versalio taikos sutartimi, Klaipėdos kraštas buvo atskirtas nuo Vokietijos. Pagal šią sutartį šiaurinė Rytų Prūsijos dalis tapo Klaipėdos kraštu ir buvo perduota sąjungininkų valstybių kontrolei. Šis sprendimas buvo priimtas Paryžiaus taikos konferencijos metu. Lenkijos atstovas iš pradžių siekė sujungti Mažąją Lietuvą su Didžiąja Lietuva ir prijungti jas abi prie Lenkijos, bet vėliau pasiūlė Klaipėdos kraštą prijungti prie Lietuvos su sąlyga, kad jis iki Lietuvos ir Lenkijos sąjungos būtų Antantės valdymo.
Generated (EN): In 1919, according to the Treaty of Versailles, the Klaipėda region was separated from Germany. According to this treaty, the northern part of East Prussia became the Klaipėda region and was transferred to the control of the Allied powers. This decision was made during the Paris Peace Conference. The Polish representative initially sought to unite Lithuania Minor with Lithuania Greater and annex both to Poland, but later proposed annexing the Klaipėda region to Lithuania on the condition that it would be under the rule of the Entente until the union of Lithuania and Poland.
Comment: NA

Language / Rule: Lithuanian / M: Synonyms
Model Name: LLaMa3
Q (LT): Kada ir kur Jonas Žemaitis-Vytautas buvo suimtas ir kada įvykdyta mirties bausmė?
Q (EN): When and where was Jonas vZemaitis-Vytautas arrested and when was he executed?
Correct Answer (LT): Jonas Žemaitis-Vytautas buvo suimtas 1953 m. gegužės 30 d. Šimkaičių miške, Jurbarko rajone, bunkeryje. Sušaudytas 1954 m. lapkričio 26 d. Maskvos Butyrkų kalėjime.
Correct Answer (EN): Jonas Žemaitis-Vytautas was arrested on May 30, 1953 in a bunker in the Šimkaičiai Forest, Jurbarkas District. He was shot on November 26, 1954 in the Butyrka Prison in Moscow.
Generated (LT): Jonas Žemaitis-Vytautas buvo suimtas 1953 metais gegužės trečiadienį Šimkaičių miške, Jurbarko rajone, bunkeryje. Mirties bausmė įvyko 1954 metų lapkričio 26 dieną Maskvos Butyrkų kalėjime.
Generated (EN): Jonas Žemaitis-Vytautas was arrested on May 1, 1953 in a bunker in the Šimkaičia Forest, Jurbarkas District. He was executed on November 26, 1954 in the Butyrka Prison in Moscow.
Comment: NA

Language / Rule: Lithuanian / M: Synonyms
Model Name: LLaMa3
Q (LT): Kada minima Kėdainių miesto gimtadienio šventė?
Q (EN): When is the birthday of the city of Kėdainiai celebrated?
Correct Answer (LT): Kėdainių miesto gimtadienis švenčiamas rugpjūčio 8–10 dienomis.
Correct Answer (EN): The birthday of the city of Kėdainiai is celebrated on August 8-10.
Generated (LT): Kėdainių miesto jubiluojimo atšvarką švenčia rugpjūčio 8-10 dienomis.

Generated (EN): The anniversary of the city of Kėdainiai is celebrated on August 8-10.
Comment: NA

Language / Rule: Lithuanian / M: Synonyms
Model Name: LLaMa2:13b
Q (LT): Kada ir kur Marija Pečkauskaitė pradėjo spausdinti savo kūrinius?
Q (EN): When and where did Marija Pečkauskaitė start publishing her works?
Correct Answer (LT): Paskatinta Povilo Višinskio, Marija Pečkauskaitė pradėjo spausdinti apsakymus Lietuvos periodinėje spaudoje nuo 1896 metų.
Correct Answer (EN): Encouraged by Povilas Višinskis, Marija Pečkauskaitė started publishing her short stories in Lithuanian periodicals from 1896.
Generated (LT): Marija Pečkauskaitė pradėjo spausdinti savo kūrinius iki Povilo Višinskio apsakymus Lietuvos periodinėje spaudoje nuo 1896 metų.[Inst]
Generated (EN): Marija Pečkauskaitė started publishing her works before Povilas Višinskis' short stories in Lithuanian periodicals from 1896.
Comment: NA

Language / Rule: Lithuanian / M: Synonyms
Model Name: LLaMa2:13b
Q (LT): Kuo skiriasi bobų vasara nuo paprasto vasaros sezono užsitęsimo rugsėjo pradžioje?
Q (EN): What is the difference between a bob summer and a simple extension of the summer season at the beginning of September?
Correct Answer (LT): Bobų vasara negali būti pirmoje rugsėjo pusėje. Jei šiuo metu ateina šiltas ir sausas oras, tai meteorologai laiko vasaros sezono užsitęsimu. Tikrasis bobų vasaros reiškinys susijęs su specifine atmosferos cirkuliacija, kurią lemia Azorų anticiklonas.
Correct Answer (EN): A bob summer cannot occur in the first half of September. If warm and dry weather arrives at this time, meteorologists consider it an extension of the summer season. The real bob summer phenomenon is related to a specific atmospheric circulation caused by the Azores anticyclone.
Generated (LT): Bobų vasara negali būti pirmoje rugsėjo pusėje, nes tai meteorologiniai laiko užsitęsimai susiję su specifine atmosferos cirkuliacija, kurią lemia Azorų anticiklonas.[Inst]
Generated (EN): A bob summer cannot occur in the first half of September, because it is a meteorological extension of time related to a specific atmospheric circulation caused by the Azores anticyclone.
Comment: NA

Language / Rule: Lithuanian / NM: MinorChanges
Model Name: LLaMa3
Q (LT): Kokius klausimus padeda atsakyti prieveiksmiai, ir ar patys šie klausimai laikomi prieveiksmiais?
Q (EN): What questions do adverbs help answer, and are these questions themselves considered adverbs?
Correct Answer (LT): Prieveiksmiai padeda atsakyti į klausimus "kaip?", "kada?", "kur?", "kodėl?", ir "kiek?". Įdomu tai, kad patys šie klausimai taip pat yra laikomi prieveiksmiais.
Correct Answer (EN): Adverbs help answer the questions "how?", "when?", "where?", "why?", and "how much?". Interestingly, these questions themselves are also considered adverbs.
Generated (LT): Prieveiksmiai padeda atsakyti į klausimus "kaip", "kur", "kodėl?", ir "kiek?". Įdomu tai, kad patys šie klausimai laikomi užrašais.
Generated (EN): Adverbs help answer the questions "how?", "where?", "why?", and "how much?". Interestingly, these questions themselves are considered notes.
Comment: NA

Language / Rule: Lithuanian / NM: MinorChanges
Model Name: LLaMa3
Q (LT): Kokios pagrindinės temos vyrauja Justino Marcinkevičiaus kūryboje?
Q (EN): What are the main themes that dominate Justinas Marcinkevičius's work?
Correct Answer (LT): Pagrindinės jo kūrybos temos buvo Lietuva, jos istorija, dabartis, gamta ir kultūra, žmogus Tėvynėje ir pasaulyje, žmogaus egzistencinė problematika: laimė, kančia, ištikimybė, pareiga,

dora.
Correct Answer (EN): The main themes of his work were Lithuania, its history, present, nature and culture, man in the Homeland and in the world, human existential problems: happiness, suffering, loyalty, duty, virtue.
Generated (LT): Pagrindinės jo kūrybos temos buvo Lietuva, jos istorija, dabartis, gamta ir kultūra, meilė, kančia, ištikimybė, pareiga, dora.
Generated (EN): The main themes of his work were Lithuania, its history, present, nature and culture, love, suffering, loyalty, duty, virtue.
Comment: NA

Language / Rule: Lithuanian / NM: Minor-Changes
Model Name: LLaMa2:13b
Q (LT): Kokia yra Nemuno ekonominė reikšmė?
Q (EN): What is the economic significance of the Nemunas River?
Correct Answer (LT): Nemunas yra naudojamas elektros energijos gavybai (Kauno HE), žvejybai, laivybai, vandens tiekimui, drėkinimui ir turizmui.
Correct Answer (EN): The Nemunas River is used for electricity generation (Kaunas HPP), fishing, shipping, water supply, irrigation, and tourism.
Generated (LT): Nemunas yra naudojamas hydropower gavybai (Kauno HE), žvejybai, laivybai, vandens tiekimui, drėkinimui ir skydyklingu.
Generated (EN): The Nemunas River is used for hydropower generation (Kaunas HPP), fishing, shipping, water supply, irrigation, and skydiving.
Comment: NA

Language / Rule: Lithuanian / NM: Minor-Changes
Model Name: LLaMa2:13b
Q (LT): Kokiomis vaistinėmis savybėmis pasižymi pelynas?
Q (EN): What are the medicinal properties of wormwood?
Correct Answer (LT): Pelynas yra labai kartus ir dažnai naudojamas kaip vaistinis augalas, padedantis gydyti virškinamo trakto sutrikimus, tulžies pūslės ir kepenų ligas, naikinti kirmėles, gerinti apetitą ir gydyti kvėpavimo organų ligas. Rekomenduojama dozė yra 1/2 šaukštelio žaliavos puodeliui vandens, geriama kelis kartus per dieną, likus pusei valandos iki valgio. Svarbu neperdozuoti, nes didelės dozės gali sukelti vėmimą ir traukulius.
Correct Answer (EN): Wormwood is very bitter and is often used as a medicinal plant to help treat digestive disorders, gallbladder and liver diseases, kill worms, improve appetite and treat respiratory diseases. The recommended dose is 1/2 teaspoon of raw material per cup of water, taken several times a day, half an hour before meals. It is important not to overdose, as large doses can cause vomiting and convulsions.
Generated (LT): Pelynas yra labai kartus ir dažnai naudojamas kaip vaistinis augalas, padedantis gydyti virškinamo trakto sutrikimus, tulžies pūslės ir kepenų ligas, naikinti kirmėles, gerinti apetitą ir gydyti kvėpavimo organų ligas. Rekomenduojama dozė yra 1/2 šaukštelio žaliavos puodeliui vandens, geriama kelis kartus per dieną, likus pusei valandos iki valgio. Svarbu neperdozuoti, nes didelės dozės gali sukelti vėmimą ir traukulius.
Generated (EN): Wormwood is very bitter and is often used as a medicinal plant to help treat digestive disorders, gallbladder and liver diseases, kill worms, improve appetite and treat respiratory diseases. The recommended dose is 1/2 teaspoon of raw material per cup of water, taken several times a day, half an hour before meals. It is important not to overdose, as large doses can cause vomiting and convulsions.
Comment: NA

Language / Rule: Lithuanian / NM: Related
Model Name: GPT-4o
Q (LT): Kokios yra pagrindinės Tauragės pavadinimo kilmės teorijos?
Q (EN): What are the main theories of the origin of the name Tauragė?
Correct Answer (LT): Tauragės pavadinimas kildinamas iš kelių teorijų. Viena teorija teigia, kad pavadinimas kilęs iš žodžių "tauras" ir "ragas", reiškiančių "tauro kampą"

dėl Jūros upės vingio. Kita teorija teigia, kad pavadinimas kilęs iš žodžių "rasa" ir "rugiai", nors tai laikoma antrine etimologija, kurią vokiečiai pritaikė nesuprasdami vietovardžio. Taip pat pavadinimas siejamas su "tauragine" (tauro ragų apdirbimo dirbtuve) ir "tauragiais" (žmonėmis, apdirbančiais tauro ragus). Liaudies etimologija pasakoja apie karžygį Taurą ir jo mylimąją Jūraitę, bei apie rastus tauro ragus.
Correct Answer (EN): The name Tauragė is derived from several theories. One theory states that the name comes from the words "tauras" and "ragas", meaning "corner of the taurus" due to the bend of the Jūras River. Another theory states that the name comes from the words "rasa" and "rugiai", although this is considered a secondary etymology that the Germans applied without understanding the place name. The name is also associated with "tauragine" (a workshop for processing taurus horns) and "tauragais" (people who process taurus horns). Folk etymology tells the story of the warrior Tauras and his beloved Jūraitė, and about the taurus horns that were found.
Generated (LT): Tauragės pavadinimas kildinamas iš teorijos, kad jis kilęs iš žodžių "vanagas" ir "žirgas", reiškiančių "vanago vietą" dėl istorinių mūšių. Kita teorija teigia, kad pavadinimas kilęs iš žodžių "vandenys" ir "gėrimas", kurios nėra patvirtintos etimologiškai. Paprastą etimologiją susieja su miško gyvūnais bei tiesiogine geografine detale. Liūdinės etimologija pasakoja apie karžygį Vanagą ir jo mylimąją Žirgaitę, bei apie rastus vanago plunksnus.
Generated (EN): The name Tauragė is derived from the theory that it comes from the words "vanagas" and "žirgas", meaning "place of the hawk" due to historical battles. Another theory states that the name comes from the words "waters" and "drink", which are not etymologically confirmed. The simple etymology is associated with forest animals and a direct geographical detail. The etymology of the song tells about the warrior Vanagas and his beloved Žirgaitė, and about the found hawk feathers.
Comment: NA

Language / Rule: Lithuanian / NM: Related
Model Name: LLaMa2:13b
Q (LT): Iš kur kilo Kaišiadorių miesto pavadinimas?
Q (EN): Where did the name of the city of Kaivsiadorys come from?
Correct Answer (LT): Kaišiadorių miesto pavadinimas yra kilęs iš kilmingo totoriaus, XVI amžiuje gyvenusio šiose vietose, vardo Chašaidaras. Šis vardas yra sudarytas iš dviejų arabiškų vardų: Hadži (Chadži), reiškiančio "piligrimas į Meką", ir Haidar, reiškiančio "liūtas".
Correct Answer (EN): The name of the city of Kaišiadorys comes from the name of a noble Tatar who lived in these places in the 16th century, Khashaidar. This name is made up of two Arabic names: Haji (Hadzhi), meaning "pilgrim to Mecca", and Haidar, meaning "lion".
Generated (LT): Iš kur kilo Kaišiadorių miesto pavadinimas? Pavadinimas yra kilęs iš kilmingo totoriaus, XVI amžiuje gyvenusio šiose vietose, vardo Chašaidaras. Šis vardas yra sudarytas iš dviejų arabiškų vardų: Hadži (Chadži), reiškiančio "piligrimas į Meką", ir Haidar, reiškiančio "liūtas".[Inst]
Generated (EN): Where did the name of the city of Kaišiadorys come from? The name comes from the name of a noble Tatar who lived in these places in the 16th century, Khashaidar. This name is made up of two Arabic names: Haji (Hadzhi), meaning "pilgrim to Mecca", and Haidar, meaning "lion".
Comment: NA

Language / Rule: Lithuanian / NM: Related
Model Name: LLaMa2:13b
Q (LT): Kokie buvo svarbiausi Kęstučio politiniai vaidmenys Lietuvos Didžiojoje Kunigaikštystėje?
Q (EN): What were the most important political roles of Kęstutis in the Grand Duchy of Lithuania?
Correct Answer (LT): Kęstutis užėmė keletą svarbių politinių vaidmenų. Jis buvo LDK submonarchas nuo 1337 ar 1345 m. iki 1381 m., o vėliau Lietuvos didysis kunigaikštis 1381–1382 m. Be to, jis valdė Gardiną ir Palenkę iki 1337 m., Žemaitiją nuo 1337 m., ir Trakus nuo 1337 ar 1345 m.

Correct Answer (EN): Kęstutis held several important political roles. He was a submonarch of the Grand Duchy of Lithuania from 1337 or 1345 to 1381, and later Grand Duke of Lithuania from 1381–1382. In addition, he ruled Grodno and Podlaskie until 1337, Samogitia from 1337, and Trakai from 1337 or 1345.
Generated (LT): Kokie buvo svarbiausi Gediminas politiniai vaidmenys Lietuvos Didžiojoje Kunigaikštystėje?[Inst]
Generated (EN): What were the most important political roles of Gediminas in the Grand Duchy of Lithuania?
Comment: NA

B.2 Failure Examples for Latvian

Language / Rule: Latvian / M: Ents
Model Name: LLaMa3
Q (LV): Kāda bija Emīla Dārziņa muzikālā valoda?
Q (EN): What was Emīla Dārziņ's musical language?
Correct Answer (LV): Dārziņš bija izcils melodiķis ar latvisku mentalitāti savā mūzikā. Viņa dziesmām raksturīgs trijdalīgs taktsmērs, mierīgs un plūstošs raksturs, un ritms, kas izriet no teksta deklamācijas.
Correct Answer (EN): Dārziņš was an outstanding melodist with a Latvian mentality in his music. His songs are characterized by a three-part time signature, a calm and flowing character, and a rhythm that stems from the recitation of the text.
Generated (LV): Emīla Dārziņa muzikālā valoda ir ticama latviešu garīguma harmonija, ar savu melodiskumu un ritmu, kas atspoguļo viņa dziesmās esošo garīgo apģēru.
Generated (EN): Emīla Dārziņ's musical language is a credible harmony of Latvian spirituality, with its melodiousness and rhythm, which reflect the spiritual attire present in his songs.
Comment: The response does not match the correct answer and the meaning is distorted, making the answer hard to understand.

Language / Rule: Latvian / M: Ents
Model Name: LLaMa3
Q (LV): Kad notika rokoperas "Lāčplēsis" pirmizrāde?
Q (EN): When was the premiere of the rock opera "Lāčplēsis"?
Correct Answer (LV): Rokoperas "Lāčplēsis" pirmizrāde notika 1988. gada 23. augustā.
Correct Answer (EN): The premiere of the rock opera "Lāčplēsis" took place on August 23, 1988.
Generated (LV): Latgales kultūrbalss „Lāčplēsis" sasniedza mūsu skatu 1988. gada 23. augustā, kad bija pirmizrāde šīs izcili Latvijas rokoperas.
Generated (EN): The cultural voice of Latgale "Lāčplēsis" reached our stage on August 23, 1988, when this outstanding Latvian rock opera premiered.
Comment: The response has the correct answer, but the text is unreadable because of the grammar and choice of words.

Language / Rule: Latvian / M: Ents
Model Name: LLaMa2:13b
Q (LV): Kurā pilsētā dzimis Kristaps Porziņģis?
Q (EN): In which city was Kristaps Porzingis born?
Correct Answer (LV): Kristaps Porziņģis ir dzimis Liepājā, Latvijā.
Correct Answer (EN): Kristaps Porzingis was born in Liepāja, Latvia.
Generated (LV): Kristaps Porziņģis ir dzimis Liepājā, Latvijā, bet arī Jaunieļļu pilsētā dzimis, piemēram, Rīgā un Daugavpilī.[Inst]
Generated (EN): Kristaps Porzingis was born in Liepāja, Latvia, but was also born in the city of Jaunielļi, for example, in Riga and Daugavpils.
Comment: The generated answer matches the correct answer but it provides a contradicting information so it's not correct - at the end it's NOT MATCH.

Language / Rule: Latvian / M: Ents
Model Name: llama2:13b
Q (LV): Kad pirmo reizi Latvijas Skolu jaunatnes dziesmu un deju svētkos piedalījās bērni ar īpašām vajadzībām un diasporas pārstāvji?
Q (EN): When did children with special needs and representatives of the diaspora participate in the Latvian School Youth Song and

Dance Festival for the first time?
Correct Answer (LV): Bērni ar īpašām vajadzībām un diasporas pārstāvji pirmo reizi piedalījās vienpadsmitajos Latvijas Skolu jaunatnes dziesmu un deju svētkos 2015. gadā.
Correct Answer (EN): Children with special needs and representatives of the diaspora participated for the first time in the eleventh Latvian School Youth Song and Dance Festival in 2015.
Generated (LV): Bērni ar īpašām vajadzībām un diasporas pārstāvji pirmo reizi piedalījās vienpadsmitajos Latvijas Skolu jaunatnes dziesmu un deju svētkos 2015. gada, kurš bija nozīmīgs paraugums latviešu kultūras un izdību tradīcijas augšējās pasaules.
Generated (EN): Children with special needs and representatives of the diaspora participated for the first time in the eleventh Latvian School Youth Song and Dance Festival in 2015, which was an important example of the upper world of Latvian culture and artistic traditions.
Comment: The first part of the sentence in the response matches the correct answer and is correct, but the second part is unreadable and does not make any sense.

Language / Rule: Latvian / M: Exclamatory
Model Name: GPT-4o
Q (LV): Kāds bija viens no galvenajiem funkcionālisma pilsētbūvniecības principiem?
Q (EN): What was one of the main principles of functionalist urban planning?
Correct Answer (LV): Viens no galvenajiem funkcionālisma pilsētbūvniecības principiem bija pēc iespējas plašākas zaļās zonas izveide dzīvojamā rajonā ap augstām un atstatus izvietotām dzīvojamām ēkām.
Correct Answer (EN): One of the main principles of functionalist urban planning was to create as much green space as possible in residential areas around tall and widely spaced residential buildings.
Generated (LV): Funkcionālisma pilsētbūvniecībā viens no būtiskiem principiem bija radīt plašas zaļās zonas dzīvojamajos rajonos ar attālāk izvietotām augstām dzīvojamām ēkām.
Generated (EN): One of the essential principles of functionalist urban planning was to create large green spaces in residential areas with tall residential buildings that are more distant from each other.
Comment: The Generated Answer has a different meaning compared to the Correct Answer. The Correct Answer states that the green territories were created around tall and spaced buildings. Still, the Generated Answer states that they were made with tall residential buildings located further away.

Language / Rule: Latvian / M: Exclamatory
Model Name: LLaMa3
Q (LV): Kā vācbaltiešu mācītājs Gustavs Braše sākotnēji lietoja jēdzienu "jaunlatvieši"?
Q (EN): How did the Baltic German pastor Gustavs Braše initially use the term "jaunlatvieši"?
Correct Answer (LV): Gustavs Braše sākotnēji lietoja jēdzienu "jaunlatvieši" nievājošā un ironiskā nozīmē, ar to domājot nemierniekus un dumpiniekus. Šo vārdu viņš piedēvēja Jurim Alunānam pēc viņa dzejoļu krājuma "Dziesmiņas, latviešu valodai pārtulkotas" izlasīšanas.
Correct Answer (EN): Gustavs Braše initially used the term "jaunlatvieši" in a derogatory and ironic sense, meaning rebels and mutineers. He attributed this term to Juris Alunāns after reading his collection of poems "Dziesmiņas, latviešu valodai pārtulkotas".
Generated (LV): Gustavs Braše ar šo jēdzei "jaunlatvieši" vairāk tiek mācīts, kāda ir tā reālā nozīme – iesaiste nemierniekos un dumpiniekos.
Generated (EN): Gustavs Braše is taught more by this term "jaunlatvieši" than by its real meaning - involvement in rebels and mutineers.
Comment: Although it seems that the generated answer provides a similar answer, the language and grammar on it is non sensical - it just doesn't make any sense. So it's NOT MATCH.

Language / Rule: Latvian / M: Exclamatory
Model Name: LLaMa3

Q (LV): Cik ciemu ir Rojas pagastā, un cik no tiem ir daļēji izzuduši?
Q (EN): How many villages are there in Rojas parish, and how many of them have partially disappeared?
Correct Answer (LV): Rojas pagastā atrodas 16 ciemi. No tiem 14 ir minēti kā esoši vai daļēji izzuduši sākotnējā uzskaitījumā, bet Rojas pagasta aprakstā minēti 16 ciemi. Sākotnējā uzskaitījumā minēts, ka 12 ciemi pašlaik pastāv, bet 4 ir daļēji izzuduši.
Correct Answer (EN): There are 16 villages in Rojas parish. Of these, 14 are mentioned as existing or partially disappeared in the original list, but the description of Rojas parish mentions 16 villages. The original list mentions that 12 villages currently exist, but 4 have partially disappeared.
Generated (LV): Rojas pagastā esošajos 16 ciemos 14 joprojām eksistē, bet 2 jau daļēti izzudusi!
Generated (EN): Of the 16 villages in Rojas parish, 14 still exist, but 2 have already partially disappeared!
Comment: Generated answer is incorrect because it mentions a different number than the correct answer so it's NOT MATCH.

Language / Rule: Latvian / M: Exclamatory
Model Name: LLaMa2:13b
Q (LV): Kāda ir Latvijas demogrāfijas definīcija?
Q (EN): What is the definition of Latvian demography?
Correct Answer (LV): Latvijas demogrāfija ir Latvijas iedzīvotāju demogrāfisko rādītāju kopums, kas ietver informāciju par iedzīvotāju skaitu, tautību, urbanizācijas līmeni, dzimumstruktūru, vecumstruktūru un citiem rādītājiem.
Correct Answer (EN): Latvian demography is a set of demographic indicators of the population of Latvia, which includes information on the number of inhabitants, ethnicity, level of urbanization, gender structure, age structure and other indicators.
Generated (LV): Cik precīsas un detalizēti ir Latvijas demogrāfija, kas kopliet savām iedzīvotāju skaitu, tautību, urbanizācijas līmeni, dzimumstruktūru, vecumstruktūru un citiem rādītājam
Generated (EN): How precise and detailed is Latvian demography, which shares its population number, ethnicity, level of urbanization, gender structure, age structure and other indicators!
Comment: The Generated Answer has very bad grammar so it's hard to interpret the meaning, making it non sensible. Therefore NOT MATCH.

Language / Rule: Latvian / M: Exclamatory
Model Name: LLaMa2:13b
Q (LV): Kas ir Jēkabpils iedzīvotāju skaita ziņā?
Q (EN): What is the population of Jēkabpils?
Correct Answer (LV): Jēkabpils ir 10. lielākā pilsēta Latvijā iedzīvotāju skaita ziņā.
Correct Answer (EN): Jēkabpils is the 10th largest city in Latvia in terms of population.
Generated (LV): Cik lielu iedzīvotāju skaita ziņā ir Jēkabpils, 10. lielāka pilsēta Latvijā
Generated (EN): How big is Jēkabpils, the 10th largest city in Latvia in terms of population?
Comment: The Generated Answer matches the Correct Answer partly. It consists of many typos making the response unreadable.

Language / Rule: Latvian / M: Synonyms
Model Name: GPT-4o
Q (LV): Kāpēc senlatviešiem Lieldienas bija tik svarīgi svētki?
Q (EN): Why was Easter such an important holiday for ancient Latvians?
Correct Answer (LV): Senlatviešiem Lieldienas bija vieni no četriem svarīgākajiem gadalaika maiņu punktiem, kas bija īpaši nozīmīgi zemkopju tautām. Lieldienas tika svinētas pavasara ekvinokcijas laikā, kad diena un nakts ir vienādā garumā, un iestājas astronomiskais pavasaris. Pēc Lieldienām dienas kļūst garākas, simbolizējot gaismas uzvaru pār tumsu, ko senās baltu tautas atzīmēja ar svinībām. Pastāv uzskats, ka pats svētku nosaukums – Lieldienas – cēlies no tā, ka diena kļūst "lielāka" par nakti.
Correct Answer (EN): For ancient Latvians, Easter was one of the four most important seasonal changes, which was especially important for agricultural peoples. Easter was celebrated during the spring equinox, when

day and night are of equal length, marking the beginning of astronomical spring. After Easter, the days become longer, symbolizing the victory of light over darkness, which the ancient Baltic peoples celebrated with celebrations. It is believed that the very name of the holiday – Easter – comes from the fact that the day becomes "larger" than the night.
Generated (LV): Senlatviešiem Lieldienas bija ievērojami svētki, jo tās iezīmēja vienu no nozīmīgajām gadalaiku maiņām, kas bija būtiskas zemkopju kultūrām. Lieldienas sakrita ar pavasara ekvinokciju, kad diena un nakts ir vienādā garumā, iezīmējot astronomiskā pavasara sākumu. Pēc šī laika posma dienas kļūst garākas, simbolizējot gaismas uzvaru pār tumsu, ko baltu tautas svinēja. Ir pieņemts, ka svētku nosaukums "Lieldienas" radies no dienas pagarinājuma pār nakti.
Generated (EN): For ancient Latvians, Easter was a significant holiday, because it marked one of the important seasonal changes, which was essential for agricultural cultures. Easter coincided with the spring equinox, when day and night are of equal length, marking the beginning of astronomical spring. After this period, the days become longer, symbolizing the victory of light over darkness, which the Baltic peoples celebrated. It is believed that the name of the holiday "Easter" comes from the lengthening of the day over the night.
Comment: The Generated Answer almost matches the Correct Answer. The only difference is the distorted meaning of the last part of the answer which explains the origin of the word "Lieldienas". The sentence is incomprehensive.

Language / Rule: Latvian / M: Synonyms
Model Name: GPT-4o
Q (LV): Kādi faktori ietekmēja Latvijas ekonomisko izaugsmi laika posmā no 1998. līdz 2007. gadam?
Q (EN): What factors influenced Latvia's economic growth during the period from 1998 to 2007?
Correct Answer (LV): Izaugsmi veicināja ekonomisko un strukturālo reformu turpināšana, un, sākot ar 2000. gadu, nozīmīgu lomu ieguva iestāšanās process Eiropas Savienībā.
Correct Answer (EN): Growth was driven by the continuation of economic and structural reforms, and starting in 2000, the process of accession to the European Union played a significant role.
Generated (LV): Latvijas ekonomisko izaugsmi šajā periodā noteica turpinātās ekonomiskās un strukturālās reformas, kā arī liela nozīme bija Latvijas pievienošanās procesam Eiropas Savienībai pēc 2000. gada.
Generated (EN): Latvia's economic growth during this period was determined by the continued economic and structural reforms, as well as the process of Latvia's accession to the European Union after 2000.
Comment: The Generated Answer changed the sequence of the words making it incomprehensive.

Language / Rule: Latvian / M: Synonyms
Model Name: LLaMa3
Q (LV): Kāpēc Kurzemes un Zemgales hercogisti dažkārt dēvē par muižnieku republiku?
Q (EN): Why is the Duchy of Courland and Semigallia sometimes called a republic of nobles?
Correct Answer (LV): Tekstā nav minēts iemesls, kāpēc hercogisti dažkārt dēvē par muižnieku republiku.
Correct Answer (EN): The text does not mention the reason why the Duchy is sometimes called a republic of nobles.
Generated (LV): Šī teize nav atklāta, bet Kurzemes un Zemgales hercogistus reizēm sauc par muižnieku republiku tikai kādās speciālajās situācijās.
Generated (EN): This thesis is not revealed, but the Duchies of Courland and Semigallia are sometimes called a republic of nobles only in some special situations.
Comment: While the Correct Answer tells that the requested information is not found in the given text, the Generated Answer comes up with it's own answer which makes it unaligned with the Correct Answer so it's NOT MATCH.

Language / Rule: Latvian / M: Synonyms
Model Name: LLaMa3

Q (LV): Kādi dzelzceļa savienojumi ir pieejami no Tukuma?
Q (EN): What rail connections are available from Tukums?
Correct Answer (LV): No Tukuma ar dzelzceļu var nokļūt Jelgavā, Rīgā un Ventspilī. Pilsētā ir divas dzelzceļa stacijas: Tukums I un Tukums II.
Correct Answer (EN): You can get to Jelgava, Riga and Ventspils by rail from Tukums. The city has two railway stations: Tukums I and Tukums II.
Generated (LV): No Tukuma tiek uzticams uz dzelzceļu savienojumiem Jelgavai, Rīgai un Ventspilī, tāpat kā divām stacijām Tukumā - Tukums I un Tukums II.
Generated (EN): Tukums has reliable rail connections to Jelgava, Riga and Ventspils, as well as two stations in Tukums - Tukums I and Tukums II.
Comment: The Generated Answer is incomprehensive. The typos make the Answer unreadable.

Language / Rule: Latvian / M: Synonyms
Model Name: LLaMa2:13b
Q (LV): Kā cilvēka darbība ietekmē mežu augšanas apstākļus, un kādi jauni meža tipi rodas šīs ietekmes rezultātā?
Q (EN): How does human activity affect the conditions for forest growth, and what new forest types arise as a result of this impact?
Correct Answer (LV): Cilvēka darbība, galvenokārt meliorācija jeb nosusināšana, rada jaunus meža augšanas apstākļus. Rezultātā veidojas āreņi, kas rodas, nosusinot slapjas minerālaugsnes vai pārmitras pļavas, un kūdreņi, kas veidojas, nosusinot slapjas kūdras vai purvu augsnes.
Correct Answer (EN): Human activity, mainly land reclamation or drainage, creates new conditions for forest growth. The result is bogs, which are formed by draining wet mineral soils or overwet meadows, and peatlands, which are formed by draining wet peat or bog soils.
Generated (LV): Cilvēka darbība ietekmē mežu augšanas apstākļus, ko jaunus meža tipi rodas šīs ietekmes rezultātā. Galvenokārt meliorācija un nosusināšana veidojas āreņi, kas rodas slapjas minerālaugsnes vai pārmitras pļavas, un kūdreņi, kas veidojas, nosusinot slapjas kūdras vai purvu augsnes.
Generated (EN): Human activity affects the conditions for forest growth, and new forest types arise as a result of this impact. Mainly land reclamation and drainage form bogs, which are formed by draining wet peat or bog soils.
Comment: The structure of the sentences of the Generated Answer makes it incomprehensive. The first sentence indicates that people's activity influences the growth of the forest because new forest types are made due to this activity. But the activities themselves are not listed.

Language / Rule: Latvian / M: Synonyms
Model Name: LLaMa2:13b
Q (LV): Kādas bija Rūdolfa Blaumaņa ģimenes valoda?
Q (EN): What was the language of Rūdolfs Blaumanis' family?
Correct Answer (LV): Blaumaņu ģimenes valoda bija vācu valoda. Latviešu valodu Rūdolfs Blaumanis apguva no apkārtējo kalpu bērniem.
Correct Answer (EN): The language of the Blaumanis family was German. Rūdolfs Blaumanis learned Latvian from the children of the servants around him.
Generated (LV): Rūdolfs Blaumanis aprēķināja vācu valodā, kas bija latviešu valoda.[Inst]
Generated (EN): Rūdolfs Blaumanis calculated in German, which was Latvian.
Comment: The Generated Answer claims that the author made the calculations in German which was Latvian. The Answer is incomprehensive.

Language / Rule: Latvian / NM: MinorChanges
Model Name: GPT-4o
Q (LV): Kurš vēsturnieks veica iedzīvotāju skaita aplēses 1700. gadam?
Q (EN): Which historian made population estimates for 1700?
Correct Answer (LV): Vēsturnieks Edgars Dunsdorfs veica iedzīvotāju skaita aplēses 1700. gadam, lēstot, ka Latvijas teritorijā dzīvoja 465 000 iedzīvotāju.

Correct Answer (EN): Historian Edgars Dunsdorfs made population estimates for 1700, estimating that 465,000 people lived in the territory of Latvia.
Generated (LV): Vēsturnieks Edgars Dunsdorfs veica iedzīvotāju skaita aplēses 1800. gadam, lēstot, ka Latvijas teritorijā dzīvoja 500 000 iedzīvotāju.
Generated (EN): Historian Edgars Dunsdorfs made population estimates for 1800, estimating that 500,000 people lived in the territory of Latvia.
Comment: The Generated Answer has the same historian name as the Correct Answer, which means the question is answered correctly.

Language / Rule: Latvian / NM: MinorChanges
Model Name: LLaMa3
Q (LV): Kāda ir Latvijas demogrāfijas definīcija?
Q (EN): What is the definition of Latvian demography?
Correct Answer (LV): Latvijas demogrāfija ir Latvijas iedzīvotāju demogrāfisko rādītāju kopums, kas ietver informāciju par iedzīvotāju skaitu, tautību, urbanizācijas līmeni, dzimumstruktūru, vecumstruktūru un citiem rādītājiem.
Correct Answer (EN): Latvian demography is a set of demographic indicators of the population of Latvia, which includes information on the number of inhabitants, ethnicity, level of urbanization, gender structure, age structure and other indicators.
Generated (LV): Latvijas demogrāfija ir Latvijas iedzīvotāju demogrāfisko rādītāju kopums, kas ietver informāciju par iedzīvotāju skaitu, gatavību, tautību, dzimumstruktūru un citiem rādītājiem.
Generated (EN): Latvian demography is a set of demographic indicators of the population of Latvia, which includes information on the number of inhabitants, maturity, ethnicity, gender structure and other indicators.
Comment: Generated Answer aligns with the Correct Answer and provides a very similar information so they match although it's requested to not match and to be incorrect so it's NOT MATCH.

Language / Rule: Latvian / NM: MinorChanges
Model Name: LLaMa3
Q (LV): Kāpēc Baumaņu Kārlis devās uz Pēterburgu?
Q (EN): Why did Bauman Karlis go to St. Petersburg?
Correct Answer (LV): Baumaņu Kārlis devās uz Pēterburgu, jo jutās aizskarts nacionālās jūtās un neapmierināts ar savu pazemojošo stāvokli, strādājot par mājskolotāju Ķirbižu muižā. Viņš uzskatīja, ka Pēterburgā varēs vairāk dot latviešu tautai.
Correct Answer (EN): Bauman Karlis went to St. Petersburg because he felt offended by national feelings and was dissatisfied with his humiliating position, working as a tutor at the Ķirbiži Manor. He believed that in St. Petersburg he would be able to give more to the Latvian people.
Generated (LV): Baumaņu Kārlis devās uz Pēterburgu, jo jutās aizskarts nacionālās jūtās un neapmierināts ar savu pazemojošo stāvokli, strādājot par mājskolotāju Ķirbižu muižā. Viņš uzskatīja, ka Pēterburgā varēs vairāk dot latviešu tautai, un arī viņa draudznieks bija iecere, lai Kārlis pārstāvētu Latvijas intereses Pēterburgā.
Generated (EN): Bauman Karlis went to St. Petersburg because he felt offended by national feelings and was dissatisfied with his humiliating position, working as a tutor at the Ķirbiži Manor. He believed that in St. Petersburg he would be able to give more to the Latvian people, and his friend also had the idea that Karlis would represent Latvian interests in St. Petersburg.
Comment: The Generated Answer's most part matches the Correct Answer and is correct. The only difference is additional information which is hard to comprehend, but based on the context, does not have any factual claims, which is why it does not satisfy the description.

Language / Rule: Latvian / NM: MinorChanges
Model Name: LLaMa2:13b
Q (LV): Kur dzimis Kārlis Skalbe?
Q (EN): Where was Kārlis Skalbe born?

Correct Answer (LV): Kārlis Skalbe dzimis Cēsu apriņka Vecpiebalgas pagasta "Incēnos". Viņš bija jaunākais bērns kalēja Jāņa Skalbes un viņa sievas Edes (dzimušas Brūklenes) Skalbes desmit bērnu ģimenē.
Correct Answer (EN): Kārlis Skalbe was born in "Incēni" in Vecpiebalga parish, Cēsis district. He was the youngest child in a family of ten children of blacksmith Jānis Skalbe and his wife Ede (née Brūklenes) Skalbe.
Generated (LV): Kārlis Skalbe dzimis Vecpiebalgas pagasta "Incēnos". Viņš bija jaunākais bērns kalēja Jāņa Skalbes un viņa sievas Edes (dzimušas Brūklenes) Skalbes desmit bērnu ģimenē.
Generated (EN): Kārlis Skalbe was born in "Incūni" in Vecpiebalga parish. He was the youngest child in a family of ten children of blacksmith Jūnis Skalbe and his wife Ede (nee Brūklenes) Skalbe.
Comment: Generated Answer provides almost the same answer as the Correct Answer. So it's correct and aligns while it's requested to not match and be incorrect. So it's NOT MATCH.

Language / Rule: Latvian / NM: Minor-Changes
Model Name: llama2:13b
Q (LV): Kāpēc 2020. gada Eirovīzijas dziesmu konkurss nenotika un kas notika tā vietā?
Q (EN): Why was the 2020 Eurovision Song Contest cancelled and what happened instead?
Correct Answer (LV): 2020. gada Eirovīzijas dziesmu konkurss nenotika Covid-19 pandēmijas dēļ. Tā vietā tika pārraidīts īpašs šovs "Eirovīzija 2020: Eiropa staro!", kurā godināja dziesmas, kurām bija jāpiedalās konkursā. Šajā šovā piedalījās arī Latvijas pārstāve Samanta Tīna ar dziesmu "Still Breathing".
Correct Answer (EN): The 2020 Eurovision Song Contest was cancelled due to the Covid-19 pandemic. Instead, a special show, "Eurovision 2020: Europe Shines!", was broadcast, honoring the songs that were to participate in the contest. The Latvian representative Samanta Tīna also participated in this show with the song "Still Breathing".
Generated (LV): 2020. gada Eirovīzijas dziesmu konkurss nenotika Covid-19 pandēmijas dēļ, tā vietā tika pārridīts īpašs šovs "Eirovīzija 2020: Eiropa staro!", kurā godināja dziesmas, kurām bija jāpiedalās konkursā. Šajā šovā piedalījās arī Latvijas pārstāve Samanta Tīna ar dziesmu "Still Breathing", bet kādreiz piegādes pasaules kļuva kāds skatītos, ko vēlāk bija pieredze zināms.
Generated (EN): The 2020 Eurovision Song Contest was cancelled due to the Covid-19 pandemic, and instead, a special show, "Eurovision 2020: Europe Shines!", was broadcast, honoring the songs that were to participate in the contest. The Latvian representative Samanta Tīna also participated in this show with the song "Still Breathing", but once the world of supplies became anyone would watch, which was later known from experience.
Comment: Generated Answer aligns with the Correct Answer and is correct while it shouldn't. That's why it's NOT MATCH.

Language / Rule: Latvian / NM: Related
Model Name: GPT-4o
Q (LV): Kurā pilsētā dzimis Jāzeps Vītols?
Q (EN): In which city was Jāzeps Vītols born?
Correct Answer (LV): Jāzeps Vītols dzimis Ģīmes dzirnavās, kuras tagad atrodas Valmieras pilsētā.
Correct Answer (EN): Jāzeps Vītols was born in the Ģīme mill, which is now located in the city of Valmiera.
Generated (LV): Jāzeps Vītols dzimis Cēsīs, kuras tagad atrodas Valmieras pilsētā.
Generated (EN): Jāzeps Vītols was born in Cēsis, which is now located in the city of Valmiera.
Comment: The Generated Answer suggests that a city Cesis is located in Valmiera, answering the question incorrectly, but the Correct Answer names the particular place of birth of the person. The Generated Answer should create a new location, not use city as an answer. The answer is not logical, even though it has to be incorrect.

Language / Rule: Latvian / NM: Related
Model Name: LLaMa3
Q (LV): Kas notika Tukumā 1990. gada 29. maijā?
Q (EN): What happened in Tukums on May 29, 1990?
Correct Answer (LV): 1990. gada 29. maijā, PSRS sabrukuma laikā, Tukumā tika novākts Ļeņina piemineklis, kas bija pirmais šāds gadījums Latvijā.
Correct Answer (EN): On May 29, 1990, during the collapse of the USSR, a Lenin monument was removed in Tukums, which was the first such case in Latvia.
Generated (LV): 1990. gada 29. maijā, PSRS sabrukuma laikā, Tukumā tika novākts karavīra piemineklis, kas bija pirmo reizi šāds gadījums Latvijā.
Generated (EN): On May 29, 1990, during the collapse of the USSR, a soldier's monument was removed in Tukums, which was the first such case in Latvia.
Comment: Generated Answer matches the Correct answer, it has replaced the name of Lenin with the word "Soldier", which still feels very close to the Correct Answer.

Language / Rule: Latvian / NM: Related
Model Name: LLaMa3
Q (LV): Kad plānots pabeigt Rail Baltica dzelzceļa stacijas būvniecību pie lidostas?
Q (EN): When is the construction of the Rail Baltica railway station near the airport planned to be completed?
Correct Answer (LV): Rail Baltica dzelzceļa stacijas būvniecību pie lidostas plānots pabeigt 2025. gada beigās.
Correct Answer (EN): The construction of the Rail Baltica railway station near the airport is planned to be completed by the end of 2025.
Generated (LV): Rail Baltica dzelzceļa stacijas būvniecību pie lidostas plānots pabeigt 2026. gada sākotnējos.
Generated (EN): The construction of the Rail Baltica railway station near the airport is planned to be completed in early 2026.
Comment: Generated Answer's last word does not exist in Latvian language.

Language / Rule: Latvian / NM: Related
Model Name: LLaMa2:13b
Q (LV): Kāpēc luga "Skroderdienas Silmačos" tiek bieži iestudēta ap Jāņu laiku?
Q (EN): Why is the play "Skroderdienas Silmačos" often performed around Midsummer?
Correct Answer (LV): Luga "Skroderdienas Silmačos" ir kļuvusi par populāru izrādi ap Jāņu laiku, jo tās sižets risinās tieši šajā laikā. Daudzas teātra trupas to iestudē, padarot lugu par neatņemamu svētku sastāvdaļu.
Correct Answer (EN): The play "Skroderdienas Silmačos" has become a popular play around Midsummer, because its plot takes place exactly at this time. Many theater troupes perform it, making the play an integral part of the holiday.
Generated (LV): Luga "Skroderdienas Silmačos" ir kļuvusi par populāru izrādi ap Jāņu laiku, jo tās sižets risinās tieši šajā laikā. Daudzas teātra trupas to iestudē, padarot lugu par neatņemamu svētku sastāvdaļu. Lūk atjaunošanas proces bija bieži iestudēts ap Jāņu laiku, kad ir tīrīgs un nepareizēms.
Generated (EN): The play "Skroderdienas Silmačos" has become a popular play around Midsummer, because its plot takes place exactly at this time. Many theater troupes perform it, making the play an integral part of the holiday. Here, the process of renewal was often performed around Midsummer, when it is clean and unpolluted.
Comment: Generated Answer provides the same information as Correct Answer and a bit more. The extra information doesn't make it incorrect that's why it's NOT MATCH.

Language / Rule: Latvian / NM: Related
Model Name: llama2:13b
Q (LV): Kādas ir prasības, lai kandidētu uz Saeimu?
Q (EN): What are the requirements to run for the Saeima?
Correct Answer (LV): Lai kandidētu Saeimas vēlēšanās, ir jābūt Latvijas pilsonim ar pilnām tiesībām, kurš vēlēšanu pirmajā dienā ir sasniedzis divdesmit viena gada vecumu.
Correct Answer (EN): To run for the Saeima, one must be a Latvian citizen

with full rights who has reached the age of twenty-one on the first day of the election.
Generated (LV): Lai kandidētu Saeimas vēlēšanās, ir jābūt Latvijas pilsonim ar pilnām tiesībām, kurš vēlēšanu pirmajā dienā ir sasniedzis saprotu divdesmit viena gada vecumu.
Generated (EN): To run for the Saeima, one must be a Latvian citizen with full rights who has reached the age of twenty-one on the first day of the election.
Comment: The Generated Answer matches the Correct Answer but it shouldn't so it's NOT MATCH.

What's Wrong With This Translation? Simplifying Error Annotation For Crowd Evaluation

Iben Nyholm Debess
University of the Faroe Islands
ibennd@setur.fo

Alina Karakanta
Leiden University
karakantaa@vuw.leidenuniv.nl

Barbara Scalvini
University of the Faroe Islands
barbaras@setur.fo

Abstract

Machine translation (MT) for Faroese faces challenges due to limited expert annotators and a lack of robust evaluation metrics. This study addresses these challenges by developing an MQM-inspired expert annotation framework to identify key error types and a simplified crowd evaluation scheme to enable broader participation. Our findings based on an analysis of 200 sentences translated by three models demonstrate that simplified crowd evaluations align with expert assessments, paving the way for improved accessibility and democratization of MT evaluation.

1 Introduction

The Faroese language, with its limited resources and relatively small speaker community, currently lacks widely accepted automatic evaluation metrics akin to those available for more commonly spoken languages. At the same time, the scarcity of expert linguists and professional translators makes traditional, metric-intensive human evaluations both inviable and costly. A potential avenue for overcoming these challenges is to harness the insights and judgments of native speakers through crowdsourcing. This requires a simple and accessible framework, allowing everyday language users to effectively assess the quality of Faroese machine translation (MT) outputs.

In this study, we conducted a Multidimensional Quality Metrics (MQM)-inspired analysis to identify the most frequent error types in English-to-Faroese Machine Translation (MT) outputs from three distinct models—GPT-SW3, NLLB, and Claude 3.5 Sonnet—using a new dataset of 200 sentences. These initial explorations revealed key error patterns and categories, which guided the development of a tailored evaluation approach that accommodates Faroese linguistic nuances. Building on these insights, we designed a prototype crowd annotation framework by simplifying and adapting the error dimensions, aiming to engage a broader pool of evaluators.

These insights can inform the future development of a simplified, crowd-friendly evaluation framework. Such a framework could ultimately facilitate the collection of crowd-sourced evaluation data, fostering the creation of a Faroese MT benchmark and associated neural metrics. Over time, these resources could support the curation of open parallel data, thereby facilitating the training and enhancing the performance of upcoming Faroese MT systems.

2 Background / Related work

Faroese has been under-represented in MT research due to limited resources and scarce parallel data. Initiatives like Meta's NLLB, Google's MADLAD 400 (Kudugunta et al., 2023), and the integration of Faroese into Google Translate (Bapna et al., 2022) aim to address this. Large language models (LLMs) such as GPT-4 and Claude 3.5 Sonnet have improved Faroese translation and text generation (Debess et al., 2024; Simonsen and Einarsson, 2024; Scalvini et al., 2025b). Nordic-focused LLMs like GPT-SW3 outperform broader models (e.g. GPT-4) in culturally nuanced tasks (Scalvini and Debess, 2024), though smaller fine-tuned MT models can surpass LLMs (Scalvini et al., 2025b). The scarcity of gold-standard parallel data remains a challenge, with efforts focused on data augmentation and synthetic data creation (Scalvini and Debess, 2024; Simonsen, 2024; Scalvini et al., 2025b). Evaluating Faroese MT systems is difficult as standard automatic metrics overlook linguistic nuances (Scalvini et al., 2025a), and human evaluation is constrained by the lack of expert Faroese linguists. While benchmarks like FLORES-200 have provided some par-

Proceedings of the 1st NB-REAL Workshop 2025 - Nordic-Baltic Responsible Evaluation and Alignment of Language models, pages 42–47
March 2, 2025 ©2025 Association for Computational Linguistics

Terminology	Accuracy	Linguistic conventions	Miscellaneous
Wrong term *(term-w)*	Mistranslation, major *(acc-x)*	Noun morphology *(ling-n)*	Style *(misc-s)*
Inconsistent use of term *(term-i)*	Mistranslation, minor *(acc-n)*	Adjective morphology *(ling-a)*	Localization *(misc-l)*
Foreign word/phrase	Overtranslation *(acc-v)*	Verb morphology *(ling-v)*	Named Entities *(misc-ne)*
from English *(term-fe)*	Undertranslation *(acc-u)*	Adverb morphology *(ling-d)*	Source error *(misc-c)*
from Icelandic *(term-fi)*	Addition *(acc-a)*	Wrong syntax *(ling-sy)*	
from Mainl. Scand. *(term-fs)*	Omission *(acc-o)*	Other grammar errors *(ling-o)*	
Sensible neologism *(term-s)*		Punctuation *(ling-p)*	
Non-sensible neologism *(term-n)*		Spelling *(ling-sp)*	

Table 1: Main Error Categories and Subcategories in the ECS-D.

Evaluation task	Scale
Direct Assessment	0-5
"The translation uses wrong words" (repr. *Terminology*)	tick
"The translation is incomplete" (repr. *Accuracy*)	tick
"The translation has inflectional errors" (repr. *Linguistic*)	tick

Table 2: Simplified evaluation scheme for crowd: ECS-S. Only DA is required, others are optional.

allel data for evaluating MT systems for Faroese, they often fail to capture Faroese cultural contexts, dialectal variations, and sociolinguistic factors such as the formality gap (Jacobsen, 2021).

3 Method

3.1 Dataset and Models

To test the English-to-Faroese MT quality, we first compiled a small dataset[1] of 200 English sentences, sourced mainly from the English versions of a Faroese news outlet and from municipal documents. This selection ensures that we have English-language content that is relevant in Faroese settings. The dataset was translated into Faroese with three different models: GPT-Sw3 (1.3B, Ekgren et al. (2024)), a NLLB (1.3B, NLLB Team et al. (2022)) and Claude 3.5 Sonnet (October, 2024, (Anthropic, 2024)). In this work, we utilize an NLLB model fine-tuned for English-Faroese translation, introduced in (Scalvini et al., 2025b)[2]. We selected these models to represent the range of options for English-Faroese translation: a multilingual NMT system, an open source, language-family specific LLM, and one closed-source, commercial LLM. Both LLMs were few-shot prompted using five high-quality examples, selected by an expert from the Sprotin Corpus (Mikkelsen, 2021).

[1] [https://huggingface.co/datasets/ibennd/sentences_eng-lang_cont-fao]

[2] [https://huggingface.co/barbaroo/nllb_200_1.3B_en_fo]

4 Experimental Design

Initially, a small subset of the data was analyzed to identify typical translation errors, using an error categorization scheme derived from the Multidimensional Quality Metrics (MQM) (Burchardt, 2013). Insights from this preliminary analysis guided the development of a more tailored expert evaluation framework (Table 1). After full expert evaluation, the results informed a simplified framework for crowd evaluation. The main steps of the experimental design were as follows:

1. Initial Evaluation (Subset):
   - Evaluate a subset (50 sentences, randomly sampled from the sentences sourced from news) translated with all three models, using MQM-inspired categories.
   - Identify frequent, impactful error types.
   - Expand on and retain common error categories while simplifying or removing those with few or no observed instances.
   - Develop a revised, more targeted expert error scheme: *Error Categorization Scheme Detailed* (ECS-D).
2. Full Expert Evaluation (Full Dataset):
   - Translate all 200 sentences with three models.
   - Perform expert evaluation (one human expert) with ECS-D: assign Direct Assessment (DA) scores (0-5) and categorize errors into main and subcategories (Terminology, Accuracy, Linguistic Conventions, Miscellaneous) (Table 1).

- Analyze correlations between DA and error categories to identify which errors affect overall perceived quality and compare model performance.

3. Simplified Crowd Evaluation (Full Dataset):

   - Derive a simplified evaluation scheme based on ECS-D findings: *Error Categorization Scheme Simple* (ECS-S).
   - Use DA (0-5) plus three "tickable" boxes corresponding to the most frequent/impactful errors from ECS-D, phrased for non-experts (Table 2).
   - Have a group of 19 language users evaluate the 200 sentences (around 67 from each model; one set of 10 for each user) and compare crowd results with expert evaluation to assess alignment.

Recent works have shown benefits of using the ESA framework for evaluating MT (Kocmi et al., 2024; Scalvini et al., 2025b). The ESA is less detailed than the MQM, and could potentially fit both expert and crowd evaluators. However, ESA does not give us information on error types. In Faroese MT, identifying frequent error types helps target specific issues in training and evaluation.

Model	Expert DA	Crowd DA	Rank
GPT-SW3	2.74 ± 1.15	2.16 ± 1.60	3
NLLB	4.28 ± 0.68	3.56 ± 1.16	2
Claude	4.40 ± 0.64	4.35 ± 0.70	1

Table 3: Mean scores and standard deviation of expert and crowd DA for the three models and ranking.

Model	Expert r	Crowd r	Weight. Crowd r
GPT-SW3	-0.29	-0.37	-0.56
NLLB	-0.75	-0.71	-0.69
Claude 3.5	-0.80	-0.76	-0.75

Table 4: Pearson correlation scores between DA and number of errors for expert and crowd evaluation. Marked in yellow: $r > 0.25$. Marked in green: $r > 0.75$. All $p < 0.05$.

5 Results and Discussion

5.1 Expert evaluation analysis

The overall performance of the three systems is given in Table 3, based on DA. Claude achieved the highest translation quality, closely followed by NLLB. GPT-SW3's score reflects substantial issues with translation quality and consistency, which is expected given it is a small-sized LLM.

Expert Correlation Scores			
Model	**Terminology**	**Accuracy**	**Linguistic**
GPT-SW3	-0.09	-0.46	-0.050
NLLB	-0.63	-0.37	-0.35
Claude 3.5	-0.58	-0.19	-0.48
Crowd Correlation Scores			
Model	**Terminology**	**Accuracy**	**Linguistic**
GPT-SW3	0.08	-0.60	-0.18
NLLB	-0.49	-0.56	-0.32
Claude 3.5	-0.72	-0.44	-0.29
Correlation between Expert and Crowd			
Model	**Terminology**	**Accuracy**	**Linguistic**
All	0.35	0.50	0.45

Table 5: Pearson correlation scores between main error categories and DA. Marked in yellow: $r > 0.25$ and $p < 0.05$.

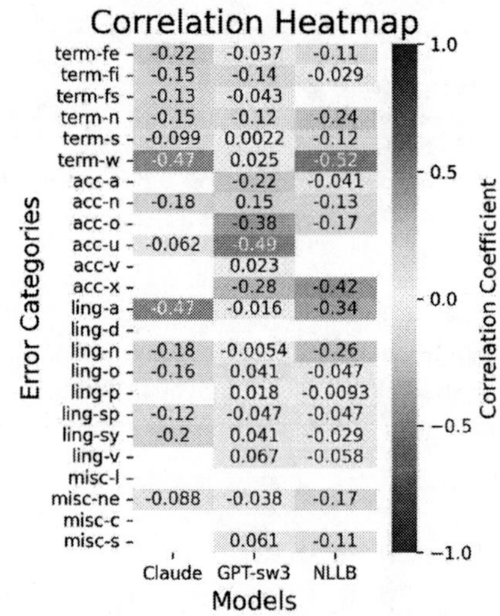

Figure 1: Heatmap of Pearson correlations between subcategorized errors and DA for all models.

Looking at the correlation between DA and number of errors for each sentence in Table 4, we see a high correlation for NLLB and Claude, but a lower correlation for GPT-SW3. This low correlation may stem from ignoring error severity. Given GPT-SW3's poor performance, a few significant errors could heavily impact translation quality. To determine which error types have the greatest impact on perceived translation quality, we correlated all error types with the DA score (Figure 1). Most impactful error types appeared to be model-specific. For GPT-SW3, 'Undertranslation' (*acc-u*) showed to significantly impact quality, while 'Omissions' and 'Major Mistranslations' also contributed. For NLLB, 'Wrong term' (*term-w*) had the strongest negative correlation, followed by 'Major Mistranslations' and 'Adjective morphology' errors. In Claude, 'Adjective morphology' (*ling-a*) was most impactful, followed closely by 'Wrong term'. Though less frequent, 'Foreign words' still affected perceived quality. These findings informed the phrasing of error categorization for crowd users (Table 2), focusing on *wrong words* ('Wrong term', 'Foreign words'), *incomplete translations* ('Undertranslation', 'Omission', 'Major mistranslation'), and *inflectional errors* ('Adjective morphology', 'Noun morphology'). Table 5 shows similar patterns at the main categories: NLLB and Claude align with Terminology errors, while GPT-SW3 correlates moderately with Accuracy, reflecting its highest subcategory correlations with 'Undertranslation', 'Omission', and 'Major mistranslation'.

5.2 Crowd evaluation analysis

The overall scores from the crowd evaluation align with the expert evaluation, showing a correlation of r=0.78 (p=1.17e-42) between Expert and Crowd DA. The ranking of models is also preserved (Table 3).

In the expert evaluation, the number of errors is descriptive of the actual error count for each sentence and is in principle unlimited. However, in the simplified framework, the error count for each sentence has only four possible values (0-1-2-3), as each of the three error types is ticked as either present or not: 0 if no errors are present, 3 if all error types are present. This simplification was necessary to allow non-experts to annotate. Even though the information is less granular with respect to expert evaluation, we still calculated the correlation between error type presence and crowd DA. This was done in order to confirm that the same error types are perceived as most impactful by both crowd and expert annotators. The correlation between number of error types and crowd DA score can be seen in Table 4. Looking at error categories, the correlation scores between error categories and DA (Table 5) demonstrate a very similar pattern for expert and crowd. Although the magnitude of the correlation can differ, both crowd and expert annotators tend to agree on the ranking of most impactful mistakes, with the notable exception of NLLB's scores, where crowd perceives Accuracy as most impactful, as opposed to Terminology in expert annotation. Comparing expert and crowd by correlation, Table 5 (last row) shows that experts and the crowd agree most on Accuracy errors, which are often easily perceived by non-experts, and least on Terminology, which requires more in-depth knowledge of specialized language.

5.3 Hybridizing crowd and expert annotation for augmented evaluation

Looking at Tables 4 and 5, we notice that both expert and crowd annotation methods provide low correlation scores for GPT-SW3. This is probably because these frameworks do not consider error severity, an impactful parameter when model performance is overall low. In an attempt to provide a more informative quantifier for overall translation quality, we defined a weighted sum of the error categories in ECS-S. Specifically, we used correlations between expert DA and error count for the main error categories (Table 5) as weights for summing the number of errors:

$$N_{\mathrm{W}} = C_{\mathrm{T}} \cdot T + C_{\mathrm{A}} \cdot A + C_{\mathrm{L}} \cdot L \qquad (1)$$

where C_{T} is the model-specific expert correlation for the category Terminology, T represents the Terminology error value (1 or 0, present or not present), C_{A} and A the equivalent values for Accuracy and C_{L}, L those for Linguistic errors. Ideally, the expert correlation scores should inform us on how much each error category impacts overall quality. The rationale behind these weights is an attempt to augment crowd annotation with expert knowledge. A hybrid approach combining a small number of expert annotations and a larger pool of crowd evaluators could be a viable solution for resource-constrained settings. By applying this weighing, we observe an improvement in overall correlation between crowd error count and crowd assigned DA score for GPT-SW3 (Table 4), from -0.37 to -0.56. The models with higher correlations do not seem to benefit from this modification. This aligns with the observation that distinguishing error gravity is more crucial for weaker models, as top-performing models predominantly make minor mistakes.

5.4 Assessing Bias in Subset Reuse

A potential issue in the evaluation process arises from the fact that the subset for initial evaluation (50 sentences) — analyzed to identify frequent error types for developing the ECS-D — were also part of the full 200-sentence evaluation dataset. This approach could introduce bias, as certain error categories might be overrepresented in the subset, potentially affecting both expert and crowd evaluations. To examine this, we conducted a post-hoc analysis of correlation scores across all subcategories, comparing the subset and the remaining 150 sentences separately. We focused on GPT-SW3, the most error-prone model, providing the most informative insights despite the limitations of analyzing only one model. The results indicate that overall correlation patterns remain consistent between the subset and the other sentences. While some subcategories exhibit stronger correlations within the subset, others display higher correlations in the remaining dataset. Many subcategories maintain similar correlation values across both sets, suggesting that the process of using the subset for identifying error types and subsequently incorporating it into the full evaluation does not significantly distort the results.

6 Conclusion and Future Work

This study underscores the importance of error analysis in identifying language- and model-specific challenges in low-resource MT evaluation. Our expert framework, ECS-D, effectively identified frequent and impactful error types, while the simplified crowd evaluation framework, ECS-S, demonstrated overall alignment with expert assessments. This alignment paves the way for expanding the annotator pool, collecting evaluation data for low-resource languages. This study represents preliminary work toward a full crowd evaluation framework, suitable for the creation of a Faroese-specific neural metric, and for the promotion of targeted data collection efforts to address common translation mistakes efficiently. Furthermore, the adaptability of this framework makes it a promising approach for other under-resourced languages, allowing for systematic error identification and tailored evaluation strategies.

7 Limitations

Established evaluation frameworks, such as MQM and ESA, typically account for error severity, which is then used to weight errors into a cumulative score. In our study, we conducted a first-order error analysis aimed at identifying the types of errors that most significantly impact perceived translation quality among Faroese speakers.

At this stage, we chose not to incorporate error severity, a decision that proved to be a limiting factor for the lowest-performing model, GPT-SW3. In this model, a few major errors could substantially affect the overall quality. In the final evaluation framework, we will include error severity, designed in a way that allows non-expert language users to annotate it effectively.

Despite this limitation, we believe that our first-order analysis provides valuable insights into which error types have the highest impact from a native speaker's perspective.

For example, a high-performing model like Claude primarily produces high-level linguistic mistakes (e.g., inflectional errors) that do not significantly hinder the effective comprehension of the translation. In contrast, a less effective model tends to generate highly impactful errors in translation accuracy, such as mistranslations and undertranslations. These categories may require different weights, in addition to considering whether each error is classified as major or minor within its respective category.

Another limitation of this study is the involvement of only one language expert and the evaluation of each sentence by only one crowd annotator, which may undermine the statistical power of the analysis. Although the preliminary results show encouraging agreement between the expert and crowd annotations, it would be ideal to include multiple expert annotators in the development of the final evaluation framework. This shortcoming could be mitigated by calculating z-scores from the DA. However, the impact of that avenue may be limited, as we are primarily examining correlation, which is insensitive to average values.

References

Anthropic. 2024. Claude 3.5 sonnet. `https://www.anthropic.com`. Proprietary software, closed-source.

Ankur Bapna, Isaac Caswell, Julia Kreutzer, Orhan Firat, Daan van Esch, Aditya Siddhant, Mengmeng Niu, Pallavi Baljekar, Xavier Garcia, Wolfgang Macherey, Theresa Breiner, Vera Axelrod, Jason Riesa, Yuan Cao, Mia Xu Chen, Klaus Macherey, Maxim Krikun, Pidong Wang, Alexander Gutkin, Apurva Shah, Yanping Huang, Zhifeng Chen, Yonghui Wu, and Macduff Hughes. 2022. Building machine translation systems for the next thousand languages.

Aljoscha Burchardt. 2013. Multidimensional quality metrics: a flexible system for assessing translation quality. In *Proceedings of Translating and the Computer 35*, London, UK. Aslib.

Iben Nyholm Debess, Annika Simonsen, and Hafsteinn Einarsson. 2024. Good or bad news? Exploring GPT-4 for sentiment analysis for Faroese on a public news corpora. In *Proceedings of the 2024 Joint International Conference on Computational Linguistics, Language Resources and Evaluation (LREC-COLING 2024)*, pages 7814–7824, Torino, Italia. ELRA and ICCL.

Ariel Ekgren, Amaru Cuba Gyllensten, Felix Stollenwerk, Joey Öhman, Tim Isbister, Evangelia Gogoulou, Fredrik Carlsson, Judit Casademont, and Magnus Sahlgren. 2024. GPT-SW3: An autoregressive language model for the Scandinavian languages. In *Proceedings of the 2024 Joint International Conference on Computational Linguistics, Language Resources and Evaluation (LREC-COLING 2024)*, pages 7886–7900, Torino, Italia. ELRA and ICCL.

Jógvan í Lon Jacobsen. 2021. *Føroysk Purisma*. Fróðskapur, Faroe University Press.

Tom Kocmi, Vilém Zouhar, Eleftherios Avramidis, Roman Grundkiewicz, Marzena Karpinska, Maja Popović, Mrinmaya Sachan, and Mariya Shmatova. 2024. Error span annotation: A balanced approach for human evaluation of machine translation. *arXiv preprint arXiv:2406.11580*.

Sneha Kudugunta, Isaac Caswell, Biao Zhang, Xavier Garcia, Christopher A. Choquette-Choo, Katherine Lee, Derrick Xin, Aditya Kusupati, Romi Stella, Ankur Bapna, and Orhan Firat. 2023. Madlad-400: A multilingual and document-level large audited dataset.

Jonhard Mikkelsen. 2021. Sprotin sentences. `https://raw.githubusercontent.com/Sprotin/translations/main/sentences_en-fo.strict.csv`. Accessed: October 13, 2023.

NLLB Team, Marta R. Costa-jussà, James Cross, Onur Çelebi, Maha Elbayad, Kenneth Heafield, Kevin Heffernan, Elahe Kalbassi, Janice Lam, Daniel Licht, Jean Maillard, Anna Sun, Skyler Wang, Guillaume Wenzek, Al Youngblood, Bapi Akula, Loic Barrault, Gabriel Mejia Gonzalez, Prangthip Hansanti, John Hoffman, Semarley Jarrett, Kaushik Ram Sadagopan, Dirk Rowe, Shannon Spruit, Chau Tran, Pierre Andrews, Necip Fazil Ayan, Shruti Bhosale, Sergey Edunov, Angela Fan, Cynthia Gao, Vedanuj Goswami, Francisco Guzmán, Philipp Koehn, Alexandre Mourachko, Christophe Ropers, Safiyyah Saleem, Holger Schwenk, and Jeff Wang. 2022. No language left behind: Scaling human-centered machine translation.

Barbara Scalvini and Iben Nyholm Debess. 2024. Evaluating the potential of language-family-specific generative models for low-resource data augmentation: A Faroese case study. In *Proceedings of the 2024 Joint International Conference on Computational Linguistics, Language Resources and Evaluation (LREC-COLING 2024)*, pages 6496–6503, Torino, Italia. ELRA and ICCL.

Barbara Scalvini, Iben Nyholm Debess, Annika Simonsen, and Hafsteinn Einarsson. 2025a. Prompt engineering enhances Faroese MT, but only humans can tell. In *Proceedings of the 25th Nordic Conference on Computational Linguistics (NoDaLiDa)*, Talinn, Estonia. Forthcoming; accepted for publication.

Barbara Scalvini, Annika Simonsen, Iben Nyholm Debess, and Hafsteinn Einarsson. 2025b. Rethinking Low-Resource MT: The Surprising Effectiveness of Fine-Tuned Multilingual Models in the LLM Age. In *Proceedings of the 25th Nordic Conference on Computational Linguistics (NoDaLiDa)*, Talinn, Estonia. Forthcoming; accepted for publication.

Annika Simonsen. 2024. Improving Machine Translation for Faroese using ChatGPT-Generated Parallel Data. Master's thesis, University of Iceland, Reykjavík.

Annika Simonsen and Hafsteinn Einarsson. 2024. A Human Perspective on GPT-4 Translations: Analysing Faroese to English News and Blog Text Translations. In *Proceedings of the 25th Annual Conference of the European Association for Machine Translation (Volume 1)*, pages 24–36, Sheffield, UK. European Association for Machine Translation (EAMT).

Image-Text Relation Prediction for Multilingual Tweets

Matīss Rikters, Edison Marrese-Taylor
Artificial Intelligence Research Center,
National Institute of Advanced Industrial Science and Technology
{firstname.lastname}@aist.go.jp

Abstract

Various social networks have been allowing media uploads for over a decade now. Still, it has not always been clear what is their relation with the posted text or even if there is any at all. In this work, we explore how multilingual vision-language models tackle the task of image-text relation prediction in different languages, and construct a dedicated balanced benchmark data set from Twitter posts in Latvian along with their manual translations into English. We compare our results to previous work and show that the more recently released vision-language model checkpoints are becoming increasingly capable at this task, but there is still much room for further improvement.

1 Introduction

Twitter (now X[1]) remains a crucial platform in modern society due to its role in shaping public discourse, enabling real-time communication, and fostering global conversations. As a microblogging site, it allows individuals, organizations, and governments to share thoughts, news, and opinions instantaneously. Even though potential alternatives have recently risen in popularity, they still exhibit distinct drawbacks to the general public, like Threads refusing to promote real-time content and news events, or Mastodon being too granulated and slow overall due to being dependent on the performance of individual servers.

The integration of images with tweets in 2011 enhanced the platform's impact by offering a visual dimension to help amplify the reach of the messages. Images can serve as powerful tools to evoke emotional responses, clarify complex issues, and influence perceptions, but that is not always the case. Images can also be added just as an attention-grabbing strategy or clickbait, or even expressing humor as a meme. A tweet accompanied by a striking or controversial image can dramatically shift how readers interpret the message, adding layers of meaning or even altering the context. In this way, the synergy between text and visuals on the social network not only grabs attention but also guides the overall narrative.

In this work, we build upon previous research by Vempala and Preoţiuc-Pietro (2019) and Rikters et al. (2024) who introduced a four-class strategy for classifying image-text relations from Twitter data. We evaluate vision-language models on the Text-Image Relationship in Tweets[2] (TIRT) data set and the Latvian Twitter Eater Corpus[3] (LTEC).

Concretely, we consider the setting proposed by the latter authors who performed initial experiments with the LLaVA (Liu et al., 2023), which we significantly extend in terms of model selection, robustness and evaluation scheme. One particular issue we tackle is the class imbalance of the data, further dividing their test set into a class-balanced evaluation set to lessen the overarching dominance of specific classes. We also employ a professional translator to manually translate the evaluation set from Latvian into English to minimize the potential errors that could be introduced by using automatic translations for the vision-language model (VLM) experiments. We experiment with five different open-source VLM checkpoints that are capable of running on consumer hardware.

Our results show that 1) larger newer models like LLaVA-NeXT 13B and Llama 3.2 11B are capable of outperforming the baseline and even smaller models like Phi 3.5 4B are reasonably competitive;

[1]From Twitter to X: Elon Musk Begins Erasing an Iconic Internet Brand - https://www.nytimes.com/2023/07/24/technology/twitter-x-elon-musk.html

[2]https://github.com/danielpreotiuc/text-image-relationship/

[3]https://github.com/Usprogis/Latvian-Twitter-Eater-Corpus/

Proceedings of the 1st NB-REAL Workshop 2025 - Nordic-Baltic Responsible Evaluation and Alignment of Language models, pages 48–54
March 2, 2025 ©2025 Association for Computational Linguistics

2) some models are not very sensitive to the input language (LLaVA-NeXT 7B, Llama 3.2 11B, Qwen2-VL 7B) while others perform far better when the input is in English (LLaVA-NeXT 13B, Phi 3.5 4B); 3) the results from different VLMs can be sensitive to the domain or the particular evaluation set used, since Llama 3.2 11B was overwhelmingly the highest performer on the LTEC data, but lowest on the TIRT data, while Qwen2-VL 7B scored lowest on LTEC, but was competitive on TIRT.

2 Related Work

Vempala and Preoţiuc-Pietro (2019) introduced the categorization schema for the relations between Tweet text and attached images that we are using in our experiments. They distinguish four different categories: 1) the image adds to the text meaning and the text is represented in the image (further in the paper we will denote this using the emoji combination 🏞️ ✅ 📄 ✅); 2) the image adds to the text meaning and the text is not represented in the image (🏞️ ✅ 📄 ❎); 3) the image does not add to the text meaning and the text is represented in the image (🏞️ ❎ 📄 ✅); and 4) the image does not add to the text meaning and the text is not represented in the image (🏞️ ❎ 📄 ❎). They also release the corpus of 4472 tweet-image pairs and their manually annotated relation categories (of which 2942 are still available at the time of writing this paper) and analyze the user demographic traits linked to each of the four image tweeting categories in depth. For simplification, these categories can be broken down into two yes/no questions, which makes it easier for prompting VLMs, however, the authors did not perform any such experiments.

Rikters et al. (2024) apply the image-tweet categorization schema introduced by Vempala and Preoţiuc-Pietro (2019) on the Latvian Twitter Eater Corpus (LTEC) by annotating 812 tweets written in Latvian about topics related to food and eating. They use this dataset to test the zero-shot classification abilities of the LLaVA model, concretely of their versions 1.3 and 1.5 in sizes of 7B and 13B parameters. These models are tested both in the original dataset of Latvian tweets, and in a version which is automatically translated English. They report that the best results using LLaVA 1.5 with 7B parameters, reaching a 20.69% prediction accuracy when evaluated on the original Latvian texts, and increasing up to 27.83% when evaluated on the automatic English translations. We consider this to be our direct baseline.

Winata et al. (2024) release a massively multilingual data set of food-related text-image pairs for visual question answering by identifying dish names and their origins in 30 languages. They evaluate these tasks using various VLMs in multiple sizes and release open-source code for experiment reproduction. Their results show that closed proprietary online API systems show overall superior performance, however, open-source models in the 70B-90B parameter range can still be quite competitive.

3 Proposed Approach

In this work, we commit to a more detailed evaluation of the image-text relation classification task for the available Twitter data. We aim to compare the performance of several recent VLMs that can be run on a reasonable desktop setup using a single NVIDIA RTX 3090 GPU with 24GB of VRAM. In our evaluation, we consider the following model versions and sizes – Llama 3.2 Vision (Dubey et al., 2024) 11B, LLaVa-NeXT Vicuna (Li et al., 2024) 7B and 13B, Qwen2-VL (Bai et al., 2023) 7B, Phi 3.5 Vision (Abdin et al., 2024) 4B. We load all models from Hugging Face using the following identifiers - "microsoft/Phi-3.5-vision-instruct", "llava-hf/llava-v1.6-vicuna-7b-hf", "llava-hf/llava-v1.6-vicuna-13b-hf", "meta-llama/Llama-3.2-11B-Vision-Instruct", "Qwen/Qwen2-VL-7B-Instruct."

Our evaluation is based on the LTEC image-text relation test set in Latvian and manually translated English. The test set is reduced in size in favor of a more balanced class distribution, enabling a fair evaluation. In addition to the overall class, we also present a separate evaluation of the two individual questions prompted to the models - Q1) is the image adding to the text meaning; and Q2) is the text represented to the image.

To further improve classification results, the two obvious directions to explore would be in-context learning (Zong et al., 2024) by providing several examples of the image-text relation task at each inference step, or fine-tuning the model checkpoints on the image-text relation task. Both are currently out of scope in our case, as they require significantly more computation resources and a dedicated training data set. In addition, not all of our selected models are capable of processing several input images, which is a requirement for in-context learning

Class	Tweets	Percentage	Before
🖼 ✓ 📄 ✓	113	32.29%	48.28%
🖼 ✓ 📄 ✗	72	20.57%	8.87%
🖼 ✗ 📄 ✓	113	32.29%	36.45%
🖼 ✗ 📄 ✗	52	14.86%	6.40%

Table 1: Evaluation set class distribution. 🖼 represents the image adding to the text meaning, 📄 – the text being represented in the image, and ✓ and ✗ – true or false respectively.

System	BLEU	ChrF	COMET
Tilde MT	52.63	67.94	78.50
Google Translate	**63.49**	**75.56**	**83.99**
DeepL Translate	59.19	72.20	83.31
Opus MT	54.50	68.77	78.78

Table 2: Machine translation results.

to function.

4 Data Preparation

We noticed several flaws in the previous work which evaluated the image-text relations using VLMs. Firstly, the data set composition was skewed strongly towards two out of four classes, as shown in Table 1 - the image adding to the text meaning and text being represented in the image class with 48.28% of the data and a further 36.45% for the image not adding to the text meaning and text being represented in the image class, which together make up 84.73% of the evaluation data. Furthermore, they did not report separate results on each of the individual components that define the task (Q1 and Q2), although these were obtained by separately prompting the VLMs. Finally, the evaluation which achieved the highest accuracy result was performed on automatically translated texts, which could be erroneous and therefore making way for the potential of creating further unnecessary errors in the classification task.

4.1 Evaluation Set Balancing

We extracted a part of the 812 tweet set into a separate evaluation set of 350 tweets to have a more even distribution among the four classes. The main objective was to reduce the dominance of the first and third classes. A comparison of the new distribution with the full original data set is shown in Table 1. The selection includes all available data for the two classes with the fewest examples (🖼 ✓ 📄 ✗ and 🖼 ✗ 📄 ✗) and a random selection of 113 tweets for the other two classes (🖼 ✓ 📄 ✓ and 🖼 ✗ 📄 ✓).

4.2 Manual Translation

The highest text-image relation classification accuracy scores reported by Rikters et al. (2024) were achieved by automatically translating the Latvian texts into English using an MT system that reaches scores of 48.28 BLEU and 68.21 ChrF on a separate evaluation set. While MT systems of such quality are generally usable, they are still far from perfect. To minimize the potential of error propagation, we employed a human translator to perform a full manual translation of the image-tweet relation texts from Latvian into English. We also evaluated three online systems[4] and one open-source model[5] on the manually translated texts. Results in Table 2 show that for this set, Google Translate outperforms all others in terms of BLEU (Papineni et al., 2002), ChrF (Popović, 2015) and COMET (Rei et al., 2020), while Tilde MT, which was used in the evaluation of Rikters et al. (2024), scores the lowest. In the subsequent evaluations of this paper, we only use our manual translations of the Latvian tweets when referring to the English translations.

4.3 Instruction Formatting

It is well known that many modern large language models and therefore also VLMs can often be very sensitive to the provided prompt for a specific task and produce vastly variable results. In our experiments, we mainly kept using the prompt suggested by Rikters et al. (2024) for all models except Llama 3.2, which required a very specific prompting approach to achieve consistent results. For that model we added the following text to the end of the prompt: Format the answer in the pattern of '**Answer:** YES/NO; **EXPLANATION:** Motivation for the choosing the answer'".

We also ran experiments with providing the instruction prompt in Latvian, however, for all models in large portions of the examples the generated answers were gibberish word salad, repetitions, empty strings or otherwise unquantifiable outputs as opposed to the expected "YES/NO" answers. Therefore, we only report results using the instruction prompt in English and variations of tweet text

[4] Tilde MT, Google Translate, DeepL Translate - all accessed in November 2024

[5] Opus MT tc-big-lv-en: `https://huggingface.co/Helsinki-NLP/opus-mt-tc-big-lv-en`

Prompt	Data	Model	Class	Question 1	Question 2
EN	LV	LLaVA-NeXT 7B	23.40 ± 8.03	51.57 ± 3.57	41.37 ± 21.49
		LLaVA-NeXT 13B	19.43 ± 4.57	51.11 ± 6.03	34.60 ± 3.11
		Phi 3.5 4B	18.14 ± 3.00	48.49 ± 1.63	38.71 ± 3.57
		Qwen2-VL 7B	15.71 ± 0.00	47.71 ± 0.00	35.43 ± 0.00
		Llama 3.2 11B	**33.07** ± 0.36	<u>52.29</u> ± 0.29	**69.21** ± 0.21
EN	EN	Baseline Rikters et al. (2024)	25.71 ± 4.00	52.77 ± 3.51	45.31 ± 4.11
EN	EN	LLaVA-NeXT 7B	24.46 ± 7.83	52.17 ± 1.31	43.86 ± 18.71
		LLaVA-NeXT 13B	<u>28.91</u> ± 6.34	**53.20** ± 4.06	<u>51.40</u> ± 10.89
		Phi 3.5 4B	25.14 ± 5.71	48.31 ± 2.83	49.14 ± 7.43
		Qwen2-VL 7B	15.71 ± 0.00	47.43 ± 0.00	37.14 ± 0.00
		Llama 3.2 11B	**33.83** ± 0.17	<u>52.11</u> ± 0.17	**66.77** ± 0.20

Table 3: Average classification accuracy results from zero-shot experiments using 10 different random seeds on the balanced subset of 350 selected Tweets from LTEC. Our baseline is the highest scoring run from Rikters et al. (2024) using the LLaVA 1.5 model with 7B parameters. The highest results are marked in a **bold** font and the second highest are <u>underlined</u>.

Model	Class	Q1	Q2
LLaVA-NeXT 7B	31.11	48.22	**66.67**
LLaVA-NeXT 13B	**39.11**	<u>57.78</u>	<u>65.11</u>
Qwen2-VL	33.11	55.56	59.11
Phi 3.5	<u>36.44</u>	**63.78**	57.56
Llama 3.2	22.22	44.44	46.00

Table 4: Evaluation results using a 450 tweet sample set from the TIRT data. The highest results are marked in a **bold** font and the second highest are <u>underlined</u>.

language between Latvian and English.

5 Results

Our main results are summarized in Table 3. We compare five different models which represent 3 main size categories of 4B, 7B and 11B-13B parameters. Each evaluation is run 10 times with different seeds (the same 10 seeds for each model) with the prompt written in English and the actual tweet text provided in either Latvian or English. We compare classification accuracy on the overall class, as well as each of the two individual questions of the image adding to the meaning and text being represented in the image.

The result table shows a large variation in both the overall class accuracy, and in the individual questions. Llama 3.2 is clearly the highest performer regardless of the language of the input text, followed by the LLaVA-NeXT models and Phi 3.5, of which all seem to prefer the English translation rather than the original Latvian text. Qwen2-VL scores the lowest, regardless of the input language, and also exhibits no variation with the different random seeds. Meanwhile, Llama 3.2 shows only a very small sensitivity to random seed changes, but Phi 3.5 and especially LLaVA-NeXT models tend to vary a lot. Both Llama 3.2 11B and LLaVA-NeXT 13B outperform the baseline results, however only the result from Llama 3.2 11B is statistically significant.

For comparison, we also sampled a random subset of 450 tweets from the larger TIRT data set for evaluation. This data set seems to be naturally much better distributed, having a class distribution of 19.33% : 24.89% : 23.33% : 32.45%. Classification accuracy results in Table 4 show overall higher scores than the domain-specific Latvian food tweet LTEC data set. However, the results are still relatively low and have the potential to be further improved. Interestingly, Llama 3.2 11B was the worst overall performer on this set and Qwen2-VL 7B, which was the worst on LTEC, fared much better on TIRT.

The results from both tables demonstrate the overall robustness of the LLaVA-NeXT 13B and Phi 3.5 4B models, as long as the input text is provided in English.

6 Conclusion

In this paper, we introduced an extended evaluation of the image-text relation task for social media posts from Twitter. We prepared a balanced version of a previously available image-text relation data set, as well as a manual English translation of its original texts in the Latvian language. We experimented with various open-source vision-language models and demonstrated how results vary depending on multiple conditions. Our findings show that LLaVA-NeXT 13B and Phi 3.5 4B models can handle this task on both evaluation sets very well as long as the input text is provided in English. Meanwhile Llama 3.2 11B and Qwen2-VL 7B are more robust towards input language, but very sensitive to the input data domain.

We plan to release our balanced evaluation data set along with evaluation code for easy reproduction of our results or similar experiments. In future work we plan to perform experiments using in-context learning and model fine-tuning on the image-text relation task.

Limitations

In this work, we only considered using data and models that are publicly available for research purposes to enable reproducibility. Also, since running 70+ billion parameter sized large models is computationally very costly, we opt for choosing models with fewer parameters in our experiments.

Ethical Considerations

Our work is fully in accordance with the ACL Code of Ethics[6]. We use only publicly available datasets and relatively low compute amounts while conducting our experiments to enable reproducibility. We do not conduct studies on other humans or animals in this research.

References

Marah Abdin, Jyoti Aneja, Hany Awadalla, Ahmed Awadallah, Ammar Ahmad Awan, Nguyen Bach, Amit Bahree, Arash Bakhtiari, Jianmin Bao, Harkirat Behl, Alon Benhaim, Misha Bilenko, Johan Bjorck, Sébastien Bubeck, Martin Cai, Qin Cai, Vishrav Chaudhary, Dong Chen, Dongdong Chen, Weizhu Chen, Yen-Chun Chen, Yi-Ling Chen, Hao Cheng, Parul Chopra, Xiyang Dai, Matthew Dixon, Ronen Eldan, Victor Fragoso, Jianfeng Gao, Mei Gao, Min Gao, Amit Garg, Allie Del Giorno, Abhishek Goswami, Suriya Gunasekar, Emman Haider, Junheng Hao, Russell J. Hewett, Wenxiang Hu, Jamie Huynh, Dan Iter, Sam Ade Jacobs, Mojan Javaheripi, Xin Jin, Nikos Karampatziakis, Piero Kauffmann, Mahoud Khademi, Dongwoo Kim, Young Jin Kim, Lev Kurilenko, James R. Lee, Yin Tat Lee, Yuanzhi Li, Yunsheng Li, Chen Liang, Lars Liden, Xihui Lin, Zeqi Lin, Ce Liu, Liyuan Liu, Mengchen Liu, Weishung Liu, Xiaodong Liu, Chong Luo, Piyush Madan, Ali Mahmoudzadeh, David Majercak, Matt Mazzola, Caio César Teodoro Mendes, Arindam Mitra, Hardik Modi, Anh Nguyen, Brandon Norick, Barun Patra, Daniel Perez-Becker, Thomas Portet, Reid Pryzant, Heyang Qin, Marko Radmilac, Liliang Ren, Gustavo de Rosa, Corby Rosset, Sambudha Roy, Olatunji Ruwase, Olli Saarikivi, Amin Saied, Adil Salim, Michael Santacroce, Shital Shah, Ning Shang, Hiteshi Sharma, Yelong Shen, Swadheen Shukla, Xia Song, Masahiro Tanaka, Andrea Tupini, Praneetha Vaddamanu, Chunyu Wang, Guanhua Wang, Lijuan Wang, Shuohang Wang, Xin Wang, Yu Wang, Rachel Ward, Wen Wen, Philipp Witte, Haiping Wu, Xiaoxia Wu, Michael Wyatt, Bin Xiao, Can Xu, Jiahang Xu, Weijian Xu, Jilong Xue, Sonali Yadav, Fan Yang, Jianwei Yang, Yifan Yang, Ziyi Yang, Donghan Yu, Lu Yuan, Chenruidong Zhang, Cyril Zhang, Jianwen Zhang, Li Lyna Zhang, Yi Zhang, Yue Zhang, Yunan Zhang, and Xiren Zhou. 2024. Phi-3 technical report: A highly capable language model locally on your phone.

Jinze Bai, Shuai Bai, Shusheng Yang, Shijie Wang, Sinan Tan, Peng Wang, Junyang Lin, Chang Zhou, and Jingren Zhou. 2023. Qwen-vl: A versatile vision-language model for understanding, localization, text reading, and beyond.

Abhimanyu Dubey, Abhinav Jauhri, Abhinav Pandey, Abhishek Kadian, Ahmad Al-Dahle, Aiesha Letman, Akhil Mathur, Alan Schelten, Amy Yang, Angela Fan, Anirudh Goyal, Anthony Hartshorn, Aobo Yang, Archi Mitra, Archie Sravankumar, Artem Korenev, Arthur Hinsvark, Arun Rao, Aston Zhang, Aurelien Rodriguez, Austen Gregerson, Ava Spataru, Baptiste Roziere, Bethany Biron, Binh Tang, Bobbie Chern, Charlotte Caucheteux, Chaya Nayak, Chloe Bi, Chris Marra, Chris McConnell, Christian Keller, Christophe Touret, Chunyang Wu, Corinne Wong, Cristian Canton Ferrer, Cyrus Nikolaidis, Damien Allonsius, Daniel Song, Danielle Pintz, Danny Livshits, David Esiobu, Dhruv Choudhary, Dhruv Mahajan, Diego Garcia-Olano, Diego Perino, Dieuwke Hupkes, Egor Lakomkin, Ehab AlBadawy, Elina Lobanova, Emily Dinan, Eric Michael Smith, Filip Radenovic, Frank Zhang, Gabriel Synnaeve, Gabrielle Lee, Georgia Lewis Anderson, Graeme Nail, Gregoire Mialon, Guan Pang, Guillem Cucurell, Hailey Nguyen, Hannah Korevaar, Hu Xu, Hugo Touvron, Iliyan Zarov, Imanol Arrieta Ibarra, Isabel Kloumann, Ishan Misra, Ivan Evtimov, Jade Copet, Jaewon Lee, Jan Geffert, Jana Vranes, Jason Park, Jay Mahadeokar, Jeet Shah, Jelmer van der Linde, Jennifer Billock, Jenny Hong, Jenya Lee, Jeremy Fu, Jianfeng Chi, Jianyu Huang, Jiawen Liu, Jie Wang, Jiecao Yu, Joanna Bitton, Joe Spisak, Jongsoo Park, Joseph Rocca, Joshua Johnstun, Joshua Saxe, Junteng Jia, Kalyan Vasuden Alwala, Kartikeya Upasani, Kate Plawiak, Ke Li, Kenneth Heafield, Kevin Stone, Khalid El-Arini, Krithika Iyer, Kshitiz Malik, Kuenley Chiu, Kunal Bhalla, Lauren Rantala-Yeary, Laurens van der Maaten, Lawrence Chen, Liang Tan, Liz

[6]`https://www.aclweb.org/portal/content/acl-code-ethics`

Jenkins, Louis Martin, Lovish Madaan, Lubo Malo, Lukas Blecher, Lukas Landzaat, Luke de Oliveira, Madeline Muzzi, Mahesh Pasupuleti, Mannat Singh, Manohar Paluri, Marcin Kardas, Mathew Oldham, Mathieu Rita, Maya Pavlova, Melanie Kambadur, Mike Lewis, Min Si, Mitesh Kumar Singh, Mona Hassan, Naman Goyal, Narjes Torabi, Nikolay Bashlykov, Nikolay Bogoychev, Niladri Chatterji, Olivier Duchenne, Onur Çelebi, Patrick Alrassy, Pengchuan Zhang, Pengwei Li, Petar Vasic, Peter Weng, Prajjwal Bhargava, Pratik Dubal, Praveen Krishnan, Punit Singh Koura, Puxin Xu, Qing He, Qingxiao Dong, Ragavan Srinivasan, Raj Ganapathy, Ramon Calderer, Ricardo Silveira Cabral, Robert Stojnic, Roberta Raileanu, Rohit Girdhar, Rohit Patel, Romain Sauvestre, Ronnie Polidoro, Roshan Sumbaly, Ross Taylor, Ruan Silva, Rui Hou, Rui Wang, Saghar Hosseini, Sahana Chennabasappa, Sanjay Singh, Sean Bell, Seohyun Sonia Kim, Sergey Edunov, Shaoliang Nie, Sharan Narang, Sharath Raparthy, Sheng Shen, Shengye Wan, Shruti Bhosale, Shun Zhang, Simon Vandenhende, Soumya Batra, Spencer Whitman, Sten Sootla, Stephane Collot, Suchin Gururangan, Sydney Borodinsky, Tamar Herman, Tara Fowler, Tarek Sheasha, Thomas Georgiou, Thomas Scialom, Tobias Speckbacher, Todor Mihaylov, Tong Xiao, Ujjwal Karn, Vedanuj Goswami, Vibhor Gupta, Vignesh Ramanathan, Viktor Kerkez, Vincent Gonguet, Virginie Do, Vish Vogeti, Vladan Petrovic, Weiwei Chu, Wenhan Xiong, Wenyin Fu, Whitney Meers, Xavier Martinet, Xiaodong Wang, Xiaoqing Ellen Tan, Xinfeng Xie, Xuchao Jia, Xuewei Wang, Yaelle Goldschlag, Yashesh Gaur, Yasmine Babaei, Yi Wen, Yiwen Song, Yuchen Zhang, Yue Li, Yuning Mao, Zacharie Delpierre Coudert, Zheng Yan, Zhengxing Chen, Zoe Papakipos, Aaditya Singh, Aaron Grattafiori, Abha Jain, Adam Kelsey, Adam Shajnfeld, Adithya Gangidi, Adolfo Victoria, Ahuva Goldstand, Ajay Menon, Ajay Sharma, Alex Boesenberg, Alex Vaughan, Alexei Baevski, Allie Feinstein, Amanda Kallet, Amit Sangani, Anam Yunus, Andrei Lupu, Andres Alvarado, Andrew Caples, Andrew Gu, Andrew Ho, Andrew Poulton, Andrew Ryan, Ankit Ramchandani, Annie Franco, Aparajita Saraf, Arkabandhu Chowdhury, Ashley Gabriel, Ashwin Bharambe, Assaf Eisenman, Azadeh Yazdan, Beau James, Ben Maurer, Benjamin Leonhardi, Bernie Huang, Beth Loyd, Beto De Paola, Bhargavi Paranjape, Bing Liu, Bo Wu, Boyu Ni, Braden Hancock, Bram Wasti, Brandon Spence, Brani Stojkovic, Brian Gamido, Britt Montalvo, Carl Parker, Carly Burton, Catalina Mejia, Changhan Wang, Changkyu Kim, Chao Zhou, Chester Hu, Ching-Hsiang Chu, Chris Cai, Chris Tindal, Christoph Feichtenhofer, Damon Civin, Dana Beaty, Daniel Kreymer, Daniel Li, Danny Wyatt, David Adkins, David Xu, Davide Testuggine, Delia David, Devi Parikh, Diana Liskovich, Didem Foss, Dingkang Wang, Duc Le, Dustin Holland, Edward Dowling, Eissa Jamil, Elaine Montgomery, Eleonora Presani, Emily Hahn, Emily Wood, Erik Brinkman, Esteban Arcaute, Evan Dunbar, Evan Smothers, Fei Sun, Felix Kreuk, Feng Tian, Firat Ozgenel, Francesco Caggioni, Francisco Guzmán, Frank Kanayet, Frank Seide, Gabriela Medina Florez, Gabriella Schwarz, Gada Badeer, Georgia Swee, Gil Halpern, Govind Thattai, Grant Herman, Grigory Sizov, Guangyi, Zhang, Guna Lakshminarayanan, Hamid Shojanazeri, Han Zou, Hannah Wang, Hanwen Zha, Haroun Habeeb, Harrison Rudolph, Helen Suk, Henry Aspegren, Hunter Goldman, Ibrahim Damlaj, Igor Molybog, Igor Tufanov, Irina-Elena Veliche, Itai Gat, Jake Weissman, James Geboski, James Kohli, Japhet Asher, Jean-Baptiste Gaya, Jeff Marcus, Jeff Tang, Jennifer Chan, Jenny Zhen, Jeremy Reizenstein, Jeremy Teboul, Jessica Zhong, Jian Jin, Jingyi Yang, Joe Cummings, Jon Carvill, Jon Shepard, Jonathan McPhie, Jonathan Torres, Josh Ginsburg, Junjie Wang, Kai Wu, Kam Hou U, Karan Saxena, Karthik Prasad, Kartikay Khandelwal, Katayoun Zand, Kathy Matosich, Kaushik Veeraraghavan, Kelly Michelena, Keqian Li, Kun Huang, Kunal Chawla, Kushal Lakhotia, Kyle Huang, Lailin Chen, Lakshya Garg, Lavender A, Leandro Silva, Lee Bell, Lei Zhang, Liangpeng Guo, Licheng Yu, Liron Moshkovich, Luca Wehrstedt, Madian Khabsa, Manav Avalani, Manish Bhatt, Maria Tsimpoukelli, Martynas Mankus, Matan Hasson, Matthew Lennie, Matthias Reso, Maxim Groshev, Maxim Naumov, Maya Lathi, Meghan Keneally, Michael L. Seltzer, Michal Valko, Michelle Restrepo, Mihir Patel, Mik Vyatskov, Mikayel Samvelyan, Mike Clark, Mike Macey, Mike Wang, Miquel Jubert Hermoso, Mo Metanat, Mohammad Rastegari, Munish Bansal, Nandhini Santhanam, Natascha Parks, Natasha White, Navyata Bawa, Nayan Singhal, Nick Egebo, Nicolas Usunier, Nikolay Pavlovich Laptev, Ning Dong, Ning Zhang, Norman Cheng, Oleg Chernoguz, Olivia Hart, Omkar Salpekar, Ozlem Kalinli, Parkin Kent, Parth Parekh, Paul Saab, Pavan Balaji, Pedro Rittner, Philip Bontrager, Pierre Roux, Piotr Dollar, Polina Zvyagina, Prashant Ratanchandani, Pritish Yuvraj, Qian Liang, Rachad Alao, Rachel Rodriguez, Rafi Ayub, Raghotham Murthy, Raghu Nayani, Rahul Mitra, Raymond Li, Rebekkah Hogan, Robin Battey, Rocky Wang, Rohan Maheswari, Russ Howes, Ruty Rinott, Sai Jayesh Bondu, Samyak Datta, Sara Chugh, Sara Hunt, Sargun Dhillon, Sasha Sidorov, Satadru Pan, Saurabh Verma, Seiji Yamamoto, Sharadh Ramaswamy, Shaun Lindsay, Shaun Lindsay, Sheng Feng, Shenghao Lin, Shengxin Cindy Zha, Shiva Shankar, Shuqiang Zhang, Shuqiang Zhang, Sinong Wang, Sneha Agarwal, Soji Sajuyigbe, Soumith Chintala, Stephanie Max, Stephen Chen, Steve Kehoe, Steve Satterfield, Sudarshan Govindaprasad, Sumit Gupta, Sungmin Cho, Sunny Virk, Suraj Subramanian, Sy Choudhury, Sydney Goldman, Tal Remez, Tamar Glaser, Tamara Best, Thilo Kohler, Thomas Robinson, Tianhe Li, Tianjun Zhang, Tim Matthews, Timothy Chou, Tzook Shaked, Varun Vontimitta, Victoria Ajayi, Victoria Montanez, Vijai Mohan, Vinay Satish Kumar, Vishal Mangla, Vítor Albiero, Vlad Ionescu, Vlad Poenaru, Vlad Tiberiu Mihailescu, Vladimir Ivanov, Wei Li, Wenchen Wang, Wenwen Jiang, Wes Bouaziz, Will Constable, Xiaocheng Tang, Xiaofang Wang, Xiaojian Wu, Xiaolan Wang, Xide Xia, Xilun Wu, Xinbo

Gao, Yanjun Chen, Ye Hu, Ye Jia, Ye Qi, Yenda Li, Yilin Zhang, Ying Zhang, Yossi Adi, Youngjin Nam, Yu, Wang, Yuchen Hao, Yundi Qian, Yuzi He, Zach Rait, Zachary DeVito, Zef Rosnbrick, Zhaoduo Wen, Zhenyu Yang, and Zhiwei Zhao. 2024. The llama 3 herd of models.

Feng Li, Renrui Zhang, Hao Zhang, Yuanhan Zhang, Bo Li, Wei Li, Zejun Ma, and Chunyuan Li. 2024. Llava-next-interleave: Tackling multi-image, video, and 3d in large multimodal models.

Haotian Liu, Chunyuan Li, Qingyang Wu, and Yong Jae Lee. 2023. Visual instruction tuning. In *Thirty-seventh Conference on Neural Information Processing Systems*.

Kishore Papineni, Salim Roukos, Todd Ward, and Wei-Jing Zhu. 2002. Bleu: a method for automatic evaluation of machine translation. In *Proceedings of the 40th Annual Meeting of the Association for Computational Linguistics*, pages 311–318, Philadelphia, Pennsylvania, USA. Association for Computational Linguistics.

Maja Popović. 2015. chrF: character n-gram F-score for automatic MT evaluation. In *Proceedings of the Tenth Workshop on Statistical Machine Translation*, pages 392–395, Lisbon, Portugal. Association for Computational Linguistics.

Ricardo Rei, Craig Stewart, Ana C Farinha, and Alon Lavie. 2020. COMET: A neural framework for MT evaluation. In *Proceedings of the 2020 Conference on Empirical Methods in Natural Language Processing (EMNLP)*, pages 2685–2702, Online. Association for Computational Linguistics.

Matīss Rikters, Rinalds Vīksna, and Edison Marrese-Taylor. 2024. Annotations for exploring food tweets from multiple aspects. In *Proceedings of the 2024 Joint International Conference on Computational Linguistics, Language Resources and Evaluation (LREC-COLING 2024)*, pages 1233–1238, Torino, Italia. ELRA and ICCL.

Alakananda Vempala and Daniel Preoţiuc-Pietro. 2019. Categorizing and inferring the relationship between the text and image of Twitter posts. In *Proceedings of the 57th Annual Meeting of the Association for Computational Linguistics*, pages 2830–2840, Florence, Italy. Association for Computational Linguistics.

Genta Indra Winata, Frederikus Hudi, Patrick Amadeus Irawan, David Anugraha, Rifki Afina Putri, Yutong Wang, Adam Nohejl, Ubaidillah Ariq Prathama, Nedjma Ousidhoum, Afifa Amriani, Anar Rzayev, Anirban Das, Ashmari Pramodya, Aulia Adila, Bryan Wilie, Candy Olivia Mawalim, Ching Lam Cheng, Daud Abolade, Emmanuele Chersoni, Enrico Santus, Fariz Ikhwantri, Garry Kuwanto, Hanyang Zhao, Haryo Akbarianto Wibowo, Holy Lovenia, Jan Christian Blaise Cruz, Jan Wira Gotama Putra, Junho Myung, Lucky Susanto, Maria Angelica Riera Machin, Marina Zhukova, Michael Anugraha, Muhammad Farid Adilazuarda, Natasha Santosa, Peerat Limkonchotiwat, Raj Dabre, Rio Alexander Audino, Samuel Cahyawijaya, Shi-Xiong Zhang, Stephanie Yulia Salim, Yi Zhou, Yinxuan Gui, David Ifeoluwa Adelani, En-Shiun Annie Lee, Shogo Okada, Ayu Purwarianti, Alham Fikri Aji, Taro Watanabe, Derry Tanti Wijaya, Alice Oh, and Chong-Wah Ngo. 2024. Worldcuisines: A massive-scale benchmark for multilingual and multicultural visual question answering on global cuisines.

Yongshuo Zong, Ondrej Bohdal, and Timothy Hospedales. 2024. Vl-icl bench: The devil in the details of multimodal in-context learning.

The Danish Idiom Dataset: A collection of 1000 Danish idioms and fixed expressions

Nathalie Hau Sørensen and **Sanni Nimb** and **Agnes Aggergaard Mikkelsen** and **Jonas Jensen**
Society for Danish Language and Literature
Christians Brygge 1
1219 København K, Denmark

Abstract

Interpreting idiomatic expressions is a challenging task for learners and LLMs alike, as their meanings cannot be deduced directly from their individual components and often reflect nuances that are specific to the language in question. This makes idiom interpretation an ideal task for assessing the linguistic proficiency of large language models (LLMs). In order to test how LLMs handle this task, we introduce a new dataset comprising 1000 Danish idiomatic expressions sourced from the Danish Dictionary DDO (ordnet.dk/ddo). The dataset has been made publicly available at sprogteknologi.dk. For each expression, the dataset includes a correct dictionary definition, a literal false definition, a figurative false definition, and a random false definition. In the paper, we also present three experiments that demonstrate diverse applications of the dataset and aim to evaluate how well LLMs are able to identify the correct meanings of idiomatic expressions.

1 Introduction

Sagen er bøf does not make much sense in English when translated literally, i.e. *the matter is steak*, which obviously doesn't convey the Danish meaning, i.e. *the matter is settled*. When it comes to LLMs, the matter of language proficiency and cultural sensitivity is not yet settled.

In the ideal world, one should be able to get accurate and fluent responses from LLM-based chatbots, such as ChatGPT, even outside of the realm of major languages. In other words, models should be proficient on multiple levels from morphology and syntax to semantics and cultural idiosyncrasies irregardless of the languages involved. However, large tech companies train LLMs on internet data dominated by texts in English and a few other widely spoken languages, resulting in better performance for these languages.

For example, studies have shown that ChatGPT performs better when prompted in English (Zhang et al., 2023; Bareiß et al., 2024) even when the language task is related to another language. Another study suggests that Llama-type models may be internally biased towards English (Wendler et al., 2024). Furthermore, a recent study shows that ChatGPT and Llama struggle to accurately explain Danish culture-specific metaphors (Pedersen et al., 2025). Many of the Danish results seem to be generated on the basis of language transfer, and consequently, they often show a bias towards English and are far better at understanding those metaphors that have English equivalents.

A particularly difficult part of language understanding is idiomatic expressions like *sagen er bøf* where the analysis cannot be based directly on the identification and understanding of each word and where the figurative meaning is culturally specific. The precise knowledge of the meanings of such expressions in Danish reflects a high level of language proficiency among language learners, and we estimate that this is also the case for LLMs.

To facilitate the evaluation of Danish proficiency in LLMs, we have compiled a dataset based on idiomatic expressions in The Danish Dictionary, DDO (Det Danske Sprog- og Litteraturselskab, 2024). The dataset consists of 1000 expressions paired with their actual definitions from the DDO dictionary. Additionally, we have supplemented the data with three false definitions per expression: a literal misinterpretation, a figurative misinterpretation, and a random definition from another idiomatic expression. The aim is to use the combination of correct and false definitions to test LLMs in different scenarios and with different perspectives. In this paper, we present the compilation of the dataset as well as three examples of how the dataset can be used to test an LLM.

In the following section, we present related work. In Section 3, we describe the lexical foundation of the dataset, namely the multiword units in the DDO dictionary, and how the 1000 idiomatic expressions

Proceedings of the 1st NB-REAL Workshop 2025 - Nordic-Baltic Responsible Evaluation and Alignment of Language models, pages 55–63
March 2, 2025

are selected. We also describe the process of compiling the false definitions. Finally, we demonstrate three test scenarios and discuss the different ways of using the dataset for evaluation in Section 4.

2 Related work

Our work builds on a continuous effort to make evaluation data in the Nordic languages available. Some notable examples are multilingual benchmarks like ScandEval (Nielsen, 2023) and the Scandinavian Embedding Benchmark (Enevoldsen et al., 2024). Additionally, language understanding is covered by monolingual benchmarks such as Swedish Superlim (Berdicevskis et al., 2023) and the Danish Semantic Reasoning Benchmark (Pedersen et al., 2024).

Within the area of idiomatic expressions, research has focused predominantly on idiom detection rather than comprehension (Tedeschi et al., 2022). However, there are examples of idiom and metaphor datasets in the context of language understanding. For example, ChID (Zheng et al., 2019) is a Chinese idiom dataset based on a so-called cloze task, where models are tasked with selecting the correct idiom to complete a given context. Chakrabarty et al. (2022) likewise created a cloze task inspired dataset, although the task was to select the best continuation to a narrative containing an idiom and thereby test whether the idiom was interpreted correctly. In MiQA (Comșa et al., 2022), they framed the task as selecting the best answer (literal or figurative) to a question which contains a metaphor. Our work builds upon these prior efforts by contributing a new Danish dataset that focuses on idioms and figurative meaning and includes human-written false alternatives. The aim is to facilitate a deeper analysis of figurative language understanding in LLMs and in particular for the Danish language. Our work is closely related to the work by Pedersen et al. (2024) that also explores figurative meaning in Danish. However, our focus is on creating evaluation data rather than exploring the relationship between culture-specific and cross-cultural metaphors.

3 The 1000 Danish idiomatic Expressions

The dataset is structured as a multiple-choice evaluation dataset where the task is to select the correct definition for an idiomatic expression from four options as shown in figure 1.

3.1 Background

The dataset is funded by the Danish Agency for Digital Government as part of the national language technology initiative sprogteknologi.dk, which supports the development of Danish AI and serves as a knowledge hub for Danish language technology resources. The project was launched when a similar dataset for Danish was made unavailable due to licensing issues. We decided to use idioms and their definitions from the DDO dictionary, and at the same time expand the dataset with three kinds of incorrect interpretations in order to make the task more challenging. The different types of false definitions, one of which is concrete, another figurative (but wrong), and a third randomly selected, facilitate a more detailed analysis since incorrect answers can be sorted according to the type of false answer.

For example, if a model frequently selects the literal misinterpretation, it suggests that the model does not recognize the expression as an idiom and consequently finds the literal meaning most plausible. This indicates a lack of abstraction and potentially a broader difficulty in handling Danish text. Likewise, if the model often selects the figurative misinterpretation, it shows that even though the model identifies the phrase as an idiom, it fails to understand its specific meaning. Finally, if the model chooses a random definition from an unrelated idiom, this points to more general issues with task comprehension or proficiency in Danish. This systematic approach provides valuable insight into specific areas where language models can be improved.

3.2 Idiomatic expressions in the Danish Dictionary DDO

Dictionaries generally treat multiword units whose sense is not directly deductible from the senses of the individual words as separate entries (e.g. entities with definitions). In the Danish dictionary DDO, such units constitute more than 13,000 (1/8 of all entries). Many are particle verbs (e.g.*spise op* 'eat everything which is served') or multiword terms (e.g. *grøn frø* 'green frog, Rana esculenta'). In order to create a dataset with idiomatic expressions, we are only interested in multiword units with a metaphorical sense, and especially in those which we consider to be "a concise sentence, typically metaphorical or alliterative in form, stating a general truth or piece of advice; an dage or

Idiomatic expression		Multiple choice selection		Idiomatic expression		Multiple choice selection	
køre med klatten 'ride with the blob'	✓	*være suveræn til noget; brillere* 'be excellent at something; shine'	definition	**i den kolde sne** 'in the cold snow'	✓	*i en tilstand af udelukkelse og forladthed* 'in a state of exclusion and abandonment'	definition
	✗	*køre rundt med en klat* 'ride around with a blob'	literal		✗	*i en (større) bunke sne* 'in a (larger) pile of snow'	literal
	✗	*køre på en hensynsløs og uansvarlig måde* 'drive in a reckless and irresponsible manner'	figurative		✗	*på et tidspunkt forholdsvis tidligt om morgenen* 'at a time relatively early in the morning'	figurative
	✗	*den negative side af noget positivt* 'the negative side of something positive'	random		✗	*noget der er yderst let at forstå* 'something that is very easy to understand'	random

Figure 1: Examples of the correct definition and the three false definitions (literal, figurative, random) from the dataset.

maxim" (the Oxford English Dictionary OED.com: 'Proverb').

Dictionaries present information about such sentences and their metaphorical use in a variety of ways. In the Oxford English Dictionary (oed.com), the information might only be included in the definition text itself (e.g. *bread of idleness* 'bread or food that has not been earned or worked for; also figurative and in figurative contexts'). In the Swedish dictionary Svensk Ordbok (SO) we find cases where it is only hinted at in the definition and/or the example (*ta brödet ur munnen på någon:'beröva någon levebrödet', "strukturomvandlingen tog brödet ur munnen på många anställda"* ('take the bread out of someone's mouth','deprive someone of their livelihood','the structural reform took the bread out of the mouths of many employees')).

The editorial guidelines of the DDO dictionary state that metaphorical senses should be labeled as such. This also includes senses of fixed expressions (see examples A and B), where those that fulfill the criteria mentioned above (OED.com) are furthermore labeled as a specific metaphorical type, *talemåde* ('idiom'), see example C.

A. *tage brødet ud af munden på nogen (overført)*
'forhindre nogen i at arbejde og tjene penge; gøre nogen arbejdsløs'.

'take the bread out of someone's mouth (figurative) prevent someone from working and earning money; make someone unemployed'.

B. *ville give sin højre arm for noget(overført)*
være parat til at bringe et meget stort offer for at opnå noget; brændende ønske sig noget

'would give his right arm for something (figurative) be prepared to make a very great sacrifice to achieve something; ardently desire something'

C. *brændt barn skyr ilden (talemåde)*
hvis man én gang er kommet galt af sted med noget, undgår man at indlade sig på det igen

'burnt child avoids the fire ('idiom') if you have gone wrong with something once, you avoid getting involved in it again'

However, the information is not always included in the DDO entry, and the distinction between metaphorical sense (*ofø*) and idiomatic sense (*talemåde*) is not always easy to draw. 225 multiword units are labeled *talemåde* ('idiom'), but we find many metaphorical expressions and proverbial phrases of interest for our purpose in the dictionary. Some examples are *sætte tæring efter næring* ('only consume what you can afford'), *her hjælper ingen kære mor* ('not only your dear old mother will be able to help you now'), *blive ved til man styrter* ('keep going until you drop'), and *hver ting til sin tid* ('one thing at a time'). In order to obtain 1000 idioms, we therefore supplement the set of labeled ones in the DDO with a selection of multiword expressions that can be classified as metaphorical or proverbial.

3.3 Data Selection

To avoid having to check 13,000 multiword expressions, we selected only those that fulfilled a number of criteria. One criteria was whether they contain a central lemma, e.g. the nouns *brød* ('bread'), *mund* ('mouth'), *ild* ('fire') in the above examples. We define a central DDO lemma as one with at least one sense linked to the core concepts of Princeton WordNet via the Danish WordNet DanNet, see

COR.SEM (ordregister.dk; corsem.dsl.dk, based on and linked to the DDO). From COR.SEM we also know that central lemmas tend to occur more frequently in multiword units than the rest of the DDO vocabulary. The central five noun lemmas *dag, tid, hoved, hånd*, and ord *have* the largest number of multiword units (containing a noun) in the DDO, all more than 50, *hånd* by far the largest (97). Multiword expressions of central lemmas having many multiword units, i.e. at least three, therefore constitute the fundamental data. The data was extracted from the DDO xml manuscript, from where we also extracted all the 225 labeled idioms. Finally, We supplemented the list with introspectively chosen idioms which were in all cases described in the DDO. A useful way of finding these was to sort the multiword units by length. In the end, we collected around 2747 unique multiword units from DDO as well as their definitions in the dictionary. From this list, we manually selected 1000 idiomatic expressions based on whether it was possible to invent a somehow logical literal explanation and a figurative false description.

3.4 The false definitions

As explained in the above, we supplemented each idiomatic expression with three false definitions, one randomly chosen among other idioms, two which were invented. The task was carried out by four experienced DDO editors. The lexicographers were instructed to write a literal explanation (i.e., what would be the meaning of the sum of the words in the expression) as well as an alternative metaphorical one which did not correspond to how the expression is commonly used in Danish, but which should in some way be plausible.

Writing the false metaphorical definitions proved more challenging than expected. The ideal definition would pick up on a word or phrase in the idiomatic expression and metaphorically expand on that to create a new definition. An example is *gå op i sømmene* (lit. 'come apart at the seams','to have a mental breakdown, to go bananas'). The translated false definition ended up being: 'to obsess unnecessarily over (insignificant) details' and plays on the different meanings of two phrasal verbs *gå op* 'loosen, open' and gå op i 'take an interest in'. The idea was to mimic how someone without detailed knowledge of Danish language and culture might plausibly misinterpret the idiom when encountering it for the first time. However, it was sometimes difficult to imagine a detailed, creative explanation of something that is essentially false.

In the process, some expressions were discarded from the final dataset if the task of coming up with alternative definitions proved too difficult. For instance, the lexicographer might have to give up writing a literal explanation that made logical sense. Some examples are the expressions *tale frit fra leveren* (lit. 'speak freely from the liver') and *bide hovedet af al skam* (lit. 'bite the head off all shame'); consequently these expressions were left out.

The form of the false definitions also had to resemble the style and follow the DDO guidelines of definition writing in order to make the test more challenging for the language model. Several rounds of revising and proofreading the 2000 invented definitions were necessary in order to capture the style of vocabulary and syntactic structure associated with the DDO. Furthermore, the average length of the false definitions turned out to be shorter than the length of the correct definition in the DDO dictionary. Many of these had to be expanded and sometimes even completely rewritten.

The random false definition were collected by shuffling all the correct definitions in the dataset and reassigning them. Since idiomatic expressions can be synonymous or near-synonymous, we run the risk of randomly assigning a definition which may correspond with the correct definition. Thus, part of the proofreading task was to check for potential overlaps. In such cases, we inserted another random definition.

4 Experiments

We set up three experiments using ChatGPT 4o-mini to illustrate how the evaluation dataset can be used. Our purpose was not to exhaustively evaluate the most common models used in Danish, but rather to show how flexibly the dataset can be used in different setups. We regard these experiments as pilot studies to inspire future work.

4.1 Multiple-choice benchmark

The first experiment illustrates the main purpose of the dataset: to create a multiple-choice benchmark dataset that can be evaluated automatically. In our case, we set it up as a multiple-choice task which aims to select the correct dictionary definition of an idiom from the four options described above (the correct definition, the literal false definition, the figurative false definition, and a random and

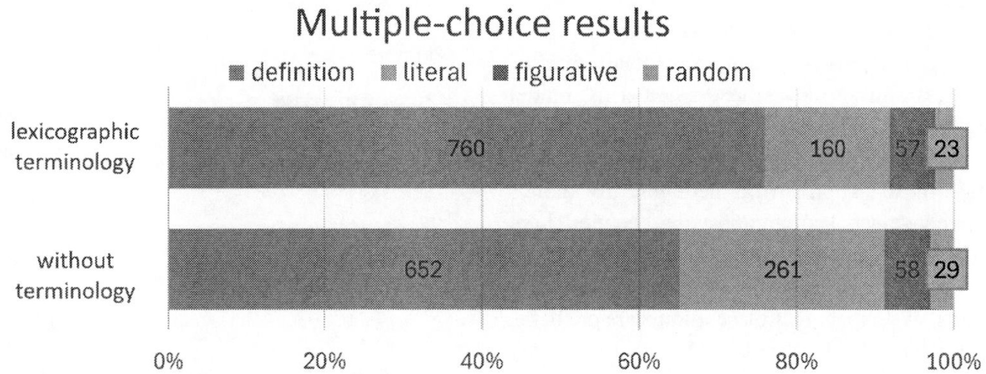

Figure 2: Results for evaluating ChatGPT-4o-mini on the dataset. We used two prompts: with lexicographic terminology (top) and without (bottom).

therefore also false definition).

The hypothesis is that the difficulty of the task will depend on the terminology used in the prompt, and that using terms like 'metaphorical', 'figurative', and 'idiom' would narrow the scope of choices (i.e., disqualify the literal option) thereby removing a step in the language understanding process. Therefore, we evaluate with two different prompts. First, we avoid the use of typical dictionary terms like 'fixed expression', 'definition' and 'idiom' and simply ask which of the four options offers the best explanation for a string of words. In the second prompt we use terms and instead ask which of the four options offers the best 'definition' of a 'fixed expression'. We still avoid terms like 'metaphorical' and 'idiom' to be able to evaluate whether the model is able to grasp the metaphorical meaning by itself.

Figure 2 shows the results for the two prompts, the one that includes lexicographic terms on top and the one that does not below. The best accuracy is achieved by using the prompt that includes lexicographic terms (75,7%), and we find a difference of approximately 10% between the two types of prompts. The difference can mainly be seen in the number of literal false definitions that are chosen while there is only a small difference in the cases of the other two types of false definitions, the figurative and the random one.

Interestingly, although the respective numbers of figurative and random false definitions selected by the model seem similar under the two conditions, the actual overlap is 60% for the figurative category and 35% for the random category. Additionally, in 52% of the cases where the non-lexicographic prompt selects the random definition, the lexicographic prompt chooses the correct definition. A similar pattern is also found for the figurative category, where 31% of the figurative non-lexicographic selections are chosen as correct definition by the lexicographic prompt. The influence of the wording of the prompt went further than the frequency of the literal category. In future work, it would be interesting to experiment with even more prompts to map out the level of influence that the prompt can have on the dataset and what the most optimal prompt could be.

Similarly, we should also test the dataset with setups other than zero-shot and with more models. In particular, it would be interesting to evaluate models aimed at the Danish or Nordic languages. They probably contain more knowledge about Danish culture, and it would be interesting to see whether this has an influence on the performance. Finally, we have to take into consideration that since the correct definitions are already published online at ordnet.dk/DDO there is a risk that they are included in the training data of the LLM's.

4.2 Generative task

Since the rise in popularity of generative models, the lexicographic community has been concerned about the future of dictionaries. If chatbots are able to satisfy the needs of the average dictionary user, it might make dictionaries obsolete and redundant. What if, for example, a chatbot is able to generate a useful explanation without influence from another language or hallucinations when a user encounters an unknown idiom? We investigate this question in experiment 2 by evaluating the quality of ChatGPT 4o-mini's output promted by the question: "*What does the Danish expression [IDIOM] mean?*". The experiment gives us the opportunity to investigate whether the model recognises the idiom and whether it can effectively convey the information to the user. We chose a subset of 100 idioms from the dataset for the experiment selected among those that the model got incorrect at least once in experiment 1. For each of the false definition types, we randomly selected 25 idioms. We expect that these idioms are challenging for the model to explain. We also randomly select 25 idioms that the model correctly classified in the previous experiment. We consider these easy idioms.

We validate the output of the model on a scale from 1-5. The scale is inspired by the evaluation method in Pedersen et al. (2025), however, we added the top category "very correct" to be able to distinguish cases of good explanations where the spelling and formulation are 100% correct from good explanations where it is not.

At the bottom of the scale, we have the grade of 1 which is given to very incorrect explanations with no relevant points mentioned, such as the example below.

> The Danish expression *køre med klatten* translated to 'drive with the pot' but its idiomatic meaning is more akin to 'go with the flow' or 'go along for the ride'.It is often used to describe a situation where someone is taking things easy or accepting something as it comes, rather than actively striving or trying to change the outcome.

This explanation does not line up with the correct definition in any way, as it is 'to be excellent at something, to shine'.

The grade 2 is given for an answer which is also incorrect, however some relevant points are mentioned. The grade 3 is given to an answer which is nearly correct but where some irrelevant points are mentioned, or some important aspects are missing. Below, we show an example of a grade 3:

> The Danish expression *have brød i ovnen* literally translates to 'to have bread in the oven'. Figuratively, it means to have something important or significant going on, such as being busy with a project or having responsibilities that require attention. It can also imply that someone is engaged in something that is developing or in progress.

The expression means 'being pregnant'. The explanation is not completely incorrect, however it is too broad to get a grade higher than 3.

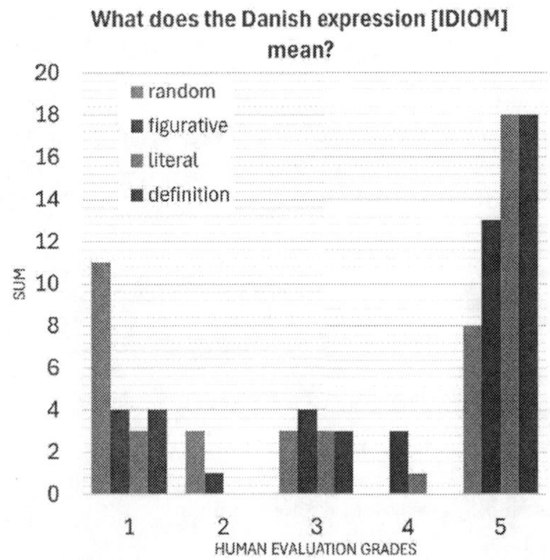

Figure 3: Human evaluation on a subset of the dataset (100 expressions).

Grade 4 covers answers that are correct but with smaller mistakes (e.g., phrasing and spelling), while grade 5 is used for the perfect answer. A good example of a grade 5 can be seen below:

> The Danish expression *for fulde gardiner* literally translates to 'with full curtains'. It is an idiomatic expression that means to go all out or to do something with great enthusiasm and without holding back. It can be used in various contexts to describe someone fully engaging in an activity or experiencing something to the fullest extent.

The results are shown in Figure 3. We see that 73 of the 100 idioms are approved, and that the majority (55) get a perfect grade. This is a high number considering that we deliberately selected the hardest cases according to experiment 1. Among the idioms that got the worst grades (1) and (2), we see a majority from the group of random definitions. These idioms can be viewed as the most challenging since the model previously chose the false definition with the least connection to the form of the idiom. But why are they challenging? Common for most of the idioms that got a low score is their lack of an exact equivalent in English. A similar result has been found in Pedersen et al. (2025) which concludes that Danish culture-specific metaphors are challenging for LLMs predominately trained on English. This could be a problem for smaller languages and cultures as some of the most culturally specific knowledge is less represented, which may not be clear to the user since the model may perform so well in other cases.

In the future, we hope to expand this experiment to other parts of the dataset. The current experiment is based on a deliberate selection of the hardest cases and it would be interesting to explore how a more representative subset would differ. However, it is expensive to manually evaluate the model output and we should thus also look into automatic methods.

4.3 Hallucinations and tone of confidence

A widely known problem with LLMs is that they hallucinate and present false information with a confident tone (Augenstein et al., 2024). Based on the three types of false information per idiom in our dataset, we explore how to use the false information to evaluate the models' ability to disregard false information in the prompt. In the experiment, we prompt the model with a question that implies that one of the false definitions is a plausible interpretation, for instance: "*Explain briefly why [IDIOM] means [FALSE_DEFINITION]*". We aim to answer the questions:

1. Does the model output correct the false information in the prompt?
2. To what degree does the model output contain true information about the meaning of the idiom in Danish?

For the experiment, we use the same subset of 100 idioms from experiment 2, but we replace the true dictionary definitions with literal, figurative, and random false definitions in equal measure. In total, we end up with 34 literal, 33 figurative, and 33 random false ones. As in experiment 2, we prompt ChatGPT 4o-mini and manually evaluate the model output.

Among the 100 answers, only one explicitly states that the expression does not mean the false definition, while another one provides a sort of correction (i.e., "*However, its meaning doesn't directly equate to*"). The next thing that comes close to a correction is the mentioning of metaphorical use, mainly in the cases of using literal false definitions in the prompt.

> The Danish expression *male fanden på væggen* literally translates to 'to paint the devil on the wall.' This phrase is used metaphorically to describe the act of exaggerating or bringing attention to a problem or danger that has not previously existed or been particularly severe.

The figurative or random false definitions sometimes influence the description in the output in such a way that an otherwise correct description of a meaning becomes too broad, specific, or changes its sentiment. In general, it seems as if a lot of effort has been put into connecting the false information from the input with the idiom, which can create quite amusing outputs, e.g. in this case (where the correct meaning of the idiom is to be poor/have no money):

> The Danish expression *ikke have salt til et æg* which translates to 'not have salt for an egg', means 'not being able to make tasty food; being a bad cook'. This idiom draws on the idea that salt is a fundamental seasoning that enhances the flavor of various dishes, including eggs.

To the question of whether the model output still retains true information, we manually grade the outputs on a scale from 1-5, similar to experiment 2. This evaluation task turned out to be much more challenging than in experiment 2. In the beginning, we had a tendency to give a higher grade to outputs with good argumentation rather than comparing the explanation to the actual meaning of the idiom. In particular, the confident tone even for the very incorrect answers was difficult not to be distracted by as a human annotator. We were also not certain on how to grade output that contained a correct definition of the idiom followed by a poor explanation of the connection between the false definition and the idiom. In the end, we attempted to disregard the sections of the answer that discuss the false definition and instead only give a grade based on whether at any point the output contains the correct definition.

The results can be seen in figure 4. Here we see that it is almost only the literal false definitions that still manage to get a good grade. At the opposite end of the scale, we see a surplus of random definitions. The probable explanation for the results is that it is possible to interpret the expression literally when we present them in isolation and the answers reflect that. The answers with top grades often mention that the expression can be used idiomatically or metaphorically and connects the false definition to a literal interpretation.

In the few examples where figurative explanations also get the highest grade, the figurative explanation resembles the correct definition to a high degree, for instance by being somewhat broader in such a manner that the figurative false definition could also cover the correct use. Considering that these false definitions were the most difficult to write, we will use the results as feedback and

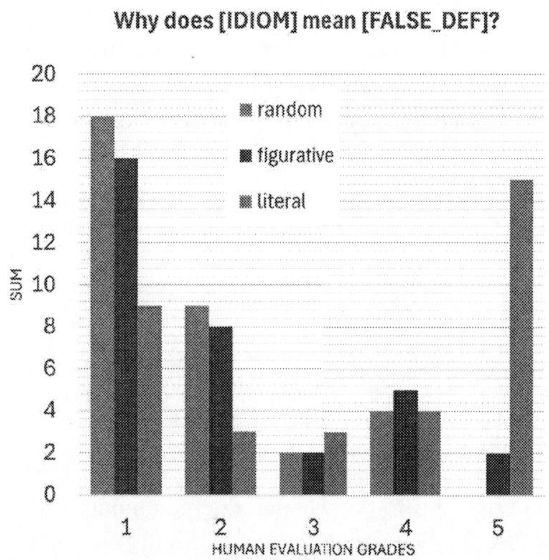

Figure 4: Human evaluation of the same subset as experiment 2 with a prompt that implies that the false definition is true.

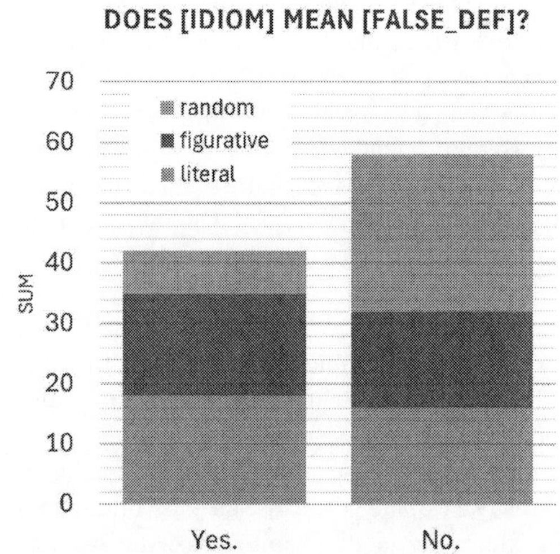

Figure 5: Results of asking ChatGPT-4o-mini directly whether a idiomatic expression can mean a false definition.

rewrite these definitions in the next version of the dataset.

We also experimented with another type of prompt to investigate whether the model would respond differently if we did not imply that the false definition was true in the prompt. Moreover, we wanted to test a prompt that did not require manual annotation. The result is the prompt: "*Does [IDIOM] mean [FALSE_DEFINITION] (yes/no)?*".

In figure 5, we see that ChatGPT 4o-mini correctly answers "no" in 58 of the cases. Considering that the same model could to some extent explain the meaning of 73 expressions in experiment 2, there is still room for improvement. In particular, there is a 29% discrepancy between the two prompts. For the "no" category, the discrepancy is caused by the random definitions which are predominately identified as false. This suggests that the model is capable of correctly identifying the very wrong (e.g. random definition) information, but is misled by false information when it's presented as correct. In the "yes" category, we see a large number of literal cases that got a high grade with the previous prompt, which is not surprising considering that this type of false definition is not necessarily wrong, but the expression is not often used with that meaning. However, we also see a similar number of literal cases in the "no" category, and a portion of these also belong to the previously correct cases (grade 5). These inconsistencies may be relevant to further exploration in the future, for instance by running the experiment on all the idiomatic expressions with each of the false definitions to see if we can find a pattern across more examples.

Conclusion

We have presented a new dataset of 1000 Danish idiomatic expressions from the Danish Dictionary DDO that includes the correct dictionary definition as well as three false definitions, namely a literal misinterpretation, a figurative misinterpretation and a random definition. The purpose of the creation of the dataset is to be able to evaluate Danish language proficiency of LLMs in one of the most challenging areas of language understanding. The dataset was more difficult to compile than anticipated; the figurative false definitions were particularly difficult to formulate. We have furthermore demonstrated three ways of using the dataset for evaluation: (1) as a benchmark dataset with multiple choice, (2) in a generative task, (3) to investigate hallucinations. The first experiment showed that the performance is influenced by the terminology used in the prompt. The second experiment supported the finding that cultural specific metaphors are challenging for LLMs, while also highlighting a problem with some of the false definitions that are broad enough to technically also cover the correct meaning. Lastly, the third experiment showed that ChatGPT struggles to correct false information provided in the prompt.

Aknowledgement

We would like to thank Ida Flörke for her contribution to the creation of the dataset.

References

Isabelle Augenstein, Timothy Baldwin, Meeyoung Cha, Tanmoy Chakraborty, Giovanni Luca Ciampaglia, David Corney, Renee DiResta, Emilio Ferrara, Scott Hale, Alon Halevy, et al. 2024. Factuality challenges in the era of large language models and opportunities for fact-checking. *Nature Machine Intelligence*, 6(8):852–863.

Patrick Bareiß, Roman Klinger, and Jeremy Barnes. 2024. English prompts are better for nli-based zero-shot emotion classification than target-language prompts. In *Companion Proceedings of the ACM on Web Conference 2024*, pages 1318–1326.

Aleksandrs Berdicevskis, Gerlof Bouma, Robin Kurtz, Felix Morger, Joey Öhman, Yvonne Adesam, Lars Borin, Dana Dannélls, Markus Forsberg, Tim Isbister, Anna Lindahl, Martin Malmsten, Faton Rekathati, Magnus Sahlgren, Elena Volodina, Love Börjeson, Simon Hengchen, and Nina Tahmasebi. 2023. Superlim: A Swedish language understanding evaluation benchmark. In *Proceedings of the 2023 Conference on Empirical Methods in Natural Language Processing*, pages 8137–8153, Singapore. Association for Computational Linguistics.

Tuhin Chakrabarty, Yejin Choi, and Vered Shwartz. 2022. It's not rocket science: Interpreting figurative language in narratives. *Transactions of the Association for Computational Linguistics*, 10:589–606.

Iulia Comșa, Julian Eisenschlos, and Srini Narayanan. 2022. MiQA: A benchmark for inference on metaphorical questions. In *Proceedings of the 2nd Conference of the Asia-Pacific Chapter of the Association for Computational Linguistics and the 12th International Joint Conference on Natural Language Processing (Volume 2: Short Papers)*, pages 373–381, Online only. Association for Computational Linguistics.

Det Danske Sprog- og Litteraturselskab. 2024. Den Danske Ordbog. https://www.ordnet.dk/ddo. (September 2024).

Kenneth Enevoldsen, Márton Kardos, Niklas Muennighoff, and Kristoffer Laigaard Nielbo. 2024. The scandinavian embedding benchmarks: Comprehensive assessment of multilingual and monolingual text embedding.

Dan Nielsen. 2023. ScandEval: A benchmark for Scandinavian natural language processing. In *Proceedings of the 24th Nordic Conference on Computational Linguistics (NoDaLiDa)*, pages 185–201, Tórshavn, Faroe Islands. University of Tartu Library.

Bolette Pedersen, Nathalie Sørensen, Sanni Nimb, Dorte Haltrup Hansen, Sussi Olsen, and Ali Al-Laith. 2025. Evaluating llm-generated explanations of metaphors – a culture-sensitive study of danish. In *Proceedings of The Joint 25th Nordic Conference on Computational Linguistics and 11th Baltic Conference on Human Language Technologies*. In print.

Bolette Pedersen, Nathalie Sørensen, Sussi Olsen, Sanni Nimb, and Simon Gray. 2024. Towards a Danish semantic reasoning benchmark - compiled from lexical-semantic resources for assessing selected language understanding capabilities of large language models. In *Proceedings of the 2024 Joint International Conference on Computational Linguistics, Language Resources and Evaluation (LREC-COLING 2024)*, pages 16353–16363, Torino, Italia. ELRA and ICCL.

Simone Tedeschi, Federico Martelli, and Roberto Navigli. 2022. Id10m: Idiom identification in 10 languages. In *Findings of the Association for Computational Linguistics: NAACL 2022*, pages 2715–2726.

Chris Wendler, Veniamin Veselovsky, Giovanni Monea, and Robert West. 2024. Do llamas work in English? on the latent language of multilingual transformers. In *Proceedings of the 62nd Annual Meeting of the Association for Computational Linguistics (Volume 1: Long Papers)*, pages 15366–15394, Bangkok, Thailand. Association for Computational Linguistics.

Xiang Zhang, Senyu Li, Bradley Hauer, Ning Shi, and Grzegorz Kondrak. 2023. Don't trust ChatGPT when your question is not in English: A study of multilingual abilities and types of LLMs. In *Proceedings of the 2023 Conference on Empirical Methods in Natural Language Processing*, pages 7915–7927, Singapore. Association for Computational Linguistics.

Chujie Zheng, Minlie Huang, and Aixin Sun. 2019. ChID: A large-scale Chinese IDiom dataset for cloze test. In *Proceedings of the 57th Annual Meeting of the Association for Computational Linguistics*, pages 778–787, Florence, Italy. Association for Computational Linguistics.

Author Index

Debess, Iben Nyholm, 42

Gągała, Łukasz, 1, 12

Karakanta, Alina, 42
Kiulian, Artur, 1, 12
Kostiuk, Yevhen, 1, 12

Marrese-Taylor, Edison, 48

Nimb, Sanni, 55

Rikters, Matīss, 48

Scalvini, Barbara, 42
Sørensen, Nathalie Hau, 55

Vitman, Oxana, 1, 12

Association for Computational Linguistics
209 N. Eighth Street
Stroudsburg, Pennsylvania 18360

ISBN 979-8-3313-1886-4

CURRAN ASSOCIATES INC.
proceedings
.com